Down The Wire Road

In The Missouri Ozarks

By Fern Angus

T & I Publishing
Purdy, MO

Library of Congress Catalog Card Number 3 540 – 452

ISBN Number 0-9637913-0-3

First Printing   1992
Second Printing 1993
Third Printing   1996

Revised Printing 2004

Printed by Litho Printers, Cassville, MO.

Cover by Larry Bangle

About The Author

Fern Angus the author was born in Dallas County, Missouri and grew up in Springfield and moved to Stone County in 1929. Fern and her husband Howard Angus lived near the old Wire Road for 53 years before moving to Marionville where she lived until January 26, 2003 where she passed away. She left two surviving children Mary Lou McCutchan and David Angus who both live in the Missouri Ozarks. According to Dave and Mary Lou their mother spent much of her leisure time in pursuit of the history of the people and the Wire Road during her lifetime.

Iva and I purchased the copyrights of this book from her surviving heirs in February of 2004 in hopes to keep the legacy and story a reality for future generations.

My interest in history of the people and those who traveled the old early roads began back in 1981 when Purdy, MO my home town was having a Centennial Celebration. They were publishing a book and I added two honor pages about my family. A few pages have been added to this Wire Road book for additional information that I have acquired in my research.

The wife and I became charter members of the Genealogical Society (BCG Society) that was formed in 1990 and I was the first editor of the Ancestors Unlimited Quarterly which I composed and featured "Kinfolkin' with Ole' Kuzzin Zeke".

I was instrumental in having the name changed to include history as I feel like they go hand in hand. One purpose then was changed to include a future museum and the pursuit of a dream for our county and the BCG & H Society of today.

I have been instrumental in publishing a five year Commemorative Booklet for the society, a Cassville in the Civil War Souvenir booklet for the first Re-enactment in 1998, a Butterfield history book in 2000; and A Special Remembrance of the Trail of Tears being the most recent.

Iva Erwin and I were classmates at Purdy high school and graduated in 1957 when we were married some 45 years ago at this writing in 2004. We both share the desire to provide history for the future generations and so purchased Fern's book copyright.

Ted Wayne Roller & Iva Jean (Erwin) Roller
Rt. #1 Box 322, Purdy, MO 65734

Dedication

This book is dedicated to my late friend, Evert Lee Hair, Sr., who passed away on August 8, 1987, at the age of ninety-eight years. When I asked Evert if he knew anything about the Wire Road, he replied, "I sure do. I was born on the Wire Road, and my parents before me"

Evert L. Hair possessed a remarkable talent for storytelling. Had it not been for the occasions when he talked—and I listened— this book most likely would never have been written.

Contents

Cover by Larry Bangle

The map pictured above shows some of the old Indian trails in the state of Missouri. From south and west of St. Louis the old Wire Road, and later Interstate I-44, followed the Pikes Trail from St. Louis to Springfield. Here, the Wire Road began it's journey south and west to Ft. Smith, Arkansas, on the Ozarks Indian Trail.

The Cherokee on the Trail of Tears crossed the Mississippi at Green's Ferry near Cape Girardeau. They sometimes traveled on the old Indian Trail, or followed the Du Tisne trail on an oxbow route which ran by way of Waynesville. The Du Tisne Trail was established in 1772. From Waynesville they then followed Pike's Trail to Springfield. An intricate network of Indian trails criss-crossed the Missouri and Arkansas Ozarks.

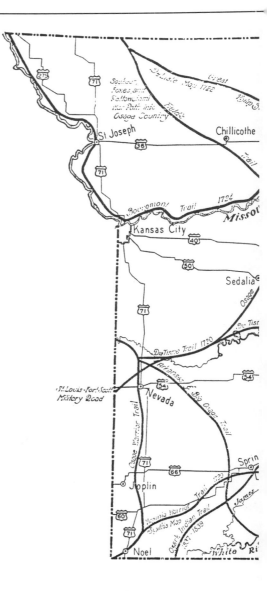

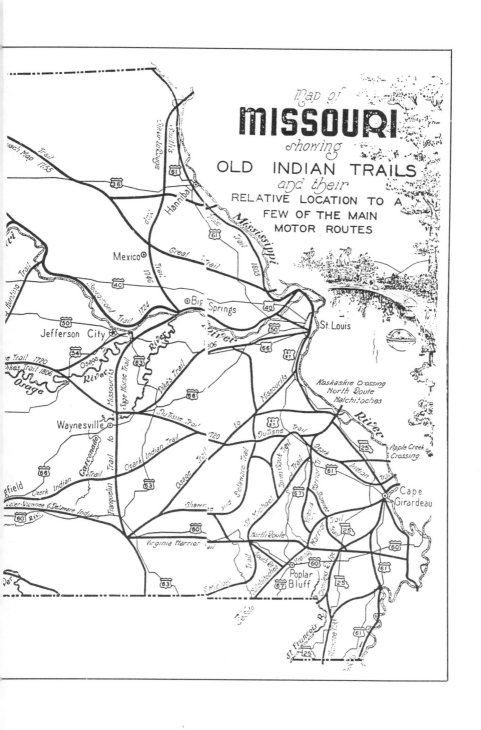

Map of
MISSOURI
showing
OLD INDIAN TRAILS
and their
RELATIVE LOCATION TO A
FEW OF THE MAIN
MOTOR ROUTES

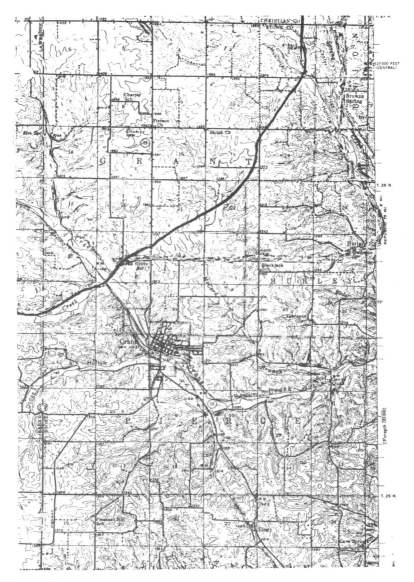

Heavy line denotes the Wire (Telegraph) Road through Stone County, Missouri.

This section of the road has been determined after much research by the author.

Chapter One

Down The Wire Road

The John Ray home in the Wilson's Creek National Battlefield Park has been restored. The Butterfield Overland Mail stopped here.

Down The Wire Road

The Wire, or Telegraph Road, winding its way through the hills and valleys of Missouri and Arkansas, is a fascinating subject to the individuals who love the history of the Ozarks region. To record its intricate past as a whole would be impossible. Pieces must be fitted together bit by bit, a scrap of information here, a colorful story there, much as the crazy patchwork quilts made by pioneer women in the olden days.

The old road, for all practical purposes, is no more. For well over a century open fields have been plowed—replowed—and harvested until almost all traces of the old trail have been obliterated. In heavily wooded areas high banks may be seen along the roadway. In almost every instance, where the roadbed is visible, large trees line the trail. With heavy, long arms reaching out, they stand like sentinels, jealously guarding the past. Scarcely a tree, or even underbrush, grows in the actual roadbed which has been packed hard by the tramping feet of men and horses.

The old road has meant various things to an untold number of people. To the thousands of Cherokee marching many miles on the ancient trail it became a road of suffering and despair—a Trail of Tears. To the daring individuals who boarded the Butterfield Overland Mail stage coaches to journey afar on what later became the Wire Road it was a road of romance and hope for the future. To the weary soldiers of both the Union and the Confederate armies it was a road to a cause considered just.

The old road today remains only a near-forgotten memory to many whose ancestors settled, reared their families, and died near the old trail. Stories handed down by word of mouth from father to son must, of necessity, be lovingly shared, recorded, and preserved lest they be lost forever in the shifting sands of time.

The Telegraph Road which passed through the Missouri Ozarks was a military project, and was designed to improve communications during the Civil War. The road began at Jefferson Barracks, St. Louis, Missouri, and continued to Ft. Smith, Arkansas Territory.

As early as 1838, Samuel F. B. Morse demonstrated his electric telegraph to the general public by sending a message over

Wire Road sign

the wires a distance of three miles. Improvements were made steadily thereafter, and the telegraph soon became the fastest method of communication. The Missouri and Western Telegraph Company, with a $1,000,000 capital was charted by the State of Missouri in 1859 to build, buy, and operate lines west of the Mississippi River. This company soon had lines in Springfield, Missouri. These, and other lines were later absorbed by the Western Union Telegraph Company.

Records from the library of the Western Union Telegraph Company contain a letter written by a Mr. Ruggles who began his telegraph career as a lineman in 1859. Mr. Ruggles worked on the first telegraph lines connecting St. Louis with the west.

The following is a quote from the letter, "In the fall of 1859, I worked at digging holes on a line between Syracuse and Springfield, Missouri. This was my first experience at construction work and it was a tough proposition. The country was rough, hilly, and full of rocks. We crossed the Osage River at Warsaw using native poles of all kinds with what we called nigger-head insulators. I did all kinds of work on the job—and then returned to set the poles. We lived in tents. H. H. Porter was our general foreman. When the weather got cold and it was snowy, work was suspended for the winter.

"We began to string the wires on the poles at Syracuse, using ladders. We next strung the second wires to Jefferson City, Missouri. The top wire on the pole was run loose for 8 or 10 poles, then tied to the nigger-head insulators. Most of the poles were of hard ash, all line-man tools were crude in those early days and consisted of one hand vise, one connector, one file, and a pair of small blocks and rope.

"After reaching Jefferson City, we met there J. J. Fry, W. R. Woodward, and a man named Slocum. Part of the gang went to Springfield to commence work on the Ft. Smith line. Another man and myself took the team. Mr. Porter left the previous fall, following the line from Syracuse to Jefferson City, doing repairing and trimming. We overtook the line gang in camp south of Springfield. The farmers delivered the poles to us, 10 or 15 at a time along the route. We had to shave them and help load them on teams which was the only means of transportation in those pioneer days. We finished setting the poles in June, 1860."

Distances along the road were marked by signs erected on the tall poles. One such sign stood on the property of Zachariah Hair, a short distance west of Brown's Spring, Missouri. The sign reading, "Springfield, 21 miles," remained standing, tall, and straight many years after the close of the Civil War. Evert L. Hair, Sr., grandson of Zachariah Hair, remembered well seeing the sign and was able to point out the exact spot where it stood.

Although communications were much improved by the construction of the telegraph lines, problems arose from time to time as sections of the line were cut or damaged. In order to eliminate the vandalism, and to stop the Rebels from firing on Union troops, the Federals adopted a policy of burning the Confederate home nearest the spot where the damage occured. Doubtless many innocent persons suffered as a result of this policy, but trouble continued many years after hostilities of the Civil War

Delaware Town sign near Nixa

ceased. Wounds, both real and imagined, were kept alive along the Missouri-Arkansas border longer than at any other place in the nation. It is estimated that 1,000 military actions took place in the area which became known as "No-man's land."

Long before the existence of the Wire Road, native Indians had established a network of trails whereby they could travel from one hunting ground to another. One trail, the Old Indian Trace, ran from St. Louis to Three Forks, Arkansas Territory. This trail was used extensively by the various tribes, and by the early Indian traders who came from the East to barter and buy Indian goods. Another trail, the White River Trace, ran westward from Green's Ferry, on the Mississippi River, to Springfield, where it turned southward to the Swan Creek Trading Post near Forsyth. The Cherokee on the Trail of Tears, 1838-1839, followed this trace from Green's Ferry to Springfield, where they then traveled the Springfield-Fayetteville Road which had been charted and surveyed

5

shortly after Greene County was organized in 1833.

As early as 1820, the Delaware Indians, having left their homes in Illinois, settled on the James River south of Springfield. William Gillis, a native of Kaskaskia, Illinois, established the James Fork Trading Post at this location in 1822. The Delaware tribes settled along the banks of the river and began a peaceful existence with the white settlers. The location became known as Delaware Town. The site of the old settlement is near present Missouri Highway 14, some four and one-half miles west of the present town of Nixa, Missouri. A new bridge now spans the James River, formerly called the St. James, at this point.

Joseph Augustine Philibert, born in St. Louis, Missouri, in 1803, was also one of the first white men to settle in this section of the Ozarks. He was employed by William Gillis at the James Fork Trading Post. Philibert, of French descent, was also an Indian trader. Information from William Earl Dotson, great-grandson of Joseph Philibert, now living in Spring Creek Valley, near Hurley, Missouri, relates that Philibert later established a trading post at the confluence of the James and White rivers near the present town of Kimberling City. Prior to the filling of Table Rock Lake, the government excavated the site of the old Philibert Post. The building, 70x150 feet, was found to be a stockade-type enclosure. Large poles set end to end, side by side, were uncovered and found to be remarkably intact after standing more than a century. The site of the Philibert Post, as well as the large farm and former home of the Dotson family, is now covered by the waters of Table Rock Lake. Joseph Philibert is buried in the Philibert Cemetery near Kimberling City, Missouri.

In 1829, a treaty was signed whereby the Delaware Indians were removed from the James River site to a Kansas reservation. With the movement of the Delaware and other tribes to western lands, Missouri was opened to a greater number of white families from Kentucky, Tennessee, Illinois, and other states.

Early counties of Missouri encompassed a much larger area than those of the present time. The following counties were once a part of Greene County, Missouri: McDonald, Newton, Jasper, Barton, Dade, Lawrence, Barry, Stone, Greene, Christian, and Webster, as well as parts of Taney, Dallas, Polk, Cedar, Vernon,

Laclede, Wright, and Douglas.

As the population of Missouri increased and small counties developed, the larger counties were divided. New road districts were formed with road commissioners elected by the property holders to oversee the operation. A county poll tax was assessed each property owner. With ready cash hard to come by, especially in the Depression years, men of the households often volunteered their services working on the county roads to pay their poll tax obligation. Cash that was collected was used to buy machinery and hire labor to maintain the roads.

With the advent of the automobile, America began a love affair with travel and better transportation that has grown continuously throughout the years and shows no sign of abating. From the time, 1908, that Henry Ford's Model T—the immortal Tin Lizzie—rolled off the assembly line, motorists demanded better roads. When the Model T ceased production in 1927, more than 15 million had been sold, some for $260, a price that seems incredibly low today. Tired of driving on roads which became impassable with each shower of rain, and disgusted with the wear and tear on their new automobiles, the population set up a hue and cry, "Get Missouri out of the mud!" which was heard by government officials in high office. As a result, Missouri began a state-wide program of road improvement which continues today.

In 1926, what seemed an impossible dream for the American motorist came true—Route 66 highway. Beginning in Chicago, Illinois, a 2,448 mile ribbon of asphalt and concrete made its way westward to Santa Monica, California. From St. Louis to Springfield, the highway followed much the same route as did the Telegraph Road. Small towns along the way—Sullivan, Cuba, St. James, Rolla, Waynesville, Lebanon, Marshfield, and others—benefited from the increased business generated by scores of travelers who were elated to be motoring on what had become known as "The road of dreams."

Bobby Troup, songwriter, and his wife were said to have been cruising down Route 66, in 1946. As the car rolled merrily along Bobby hummed a tune. This suggested to Mrs. Troup that her husband should write a song about the new highway, Route 66. The result was the hit song "Get Your Kicks On Route 66." Two

7

interesting books have been published about the old road, *Route 66. The Mother Road*, by Michael Wallis and *Route 66, The Highway and Its People*, by Quinta Scott and Susan Groce Kelley. On January 11, 1990, Governor John Ashcroft signed legislation designating the 307 miles of Route 66 in Missouri as an historical highway. An organization, The Route 66 Association of Missouri, has been formed. Signs picturing the familiar black and white shield on a brown background have been erected along the route in Missouri and other states.

Today, Interstate I-44 highway from St. Louis to Springfield, Missouri, follows much the same route as did the Old Indian Trace, the Wire Road, and Route 66. Amid the hustle and bustle of modern times, the Interstate highways hurry along, by-passing the small towns—the Main Streets of America. Regrettably, travelers miss much of the history of any given region.

Heap high the farmers wintry hoard!
Heap high the golden corn!
No richer gift has autumn poured
From out her lavish horn.

Let other lands exulting glean
The apple from the pine,
The orange from it's glossy green
The cluster from the vine.

But let the good old corn adorn
The hills our fathers trod;
Still let us for His golden corn
Send up our thanks to God.

John Greenleaf Whittier 1807-1892

Springfield-Fayetteville Road

The map on pages 10-11 includes a part of the old Springfield-Fayetteville road. The land for the road was surveyed by A. A. Jamison in January and February, 1835 under a contract issued December 17, 1834. The sub-divisions were surveyed by William C. Pride several years later. This contract was issued May 10, 1845. The document was signed by F. B. Conway, Surveyor of Public Lands in the States of Illinois and Missouri.

It is well to note that this road had already been established when the Cherokee traveled across Missouri in 1837-1838-1839. After crossing what is now the Stone-Christian County line and continuing south and west this road forked to the right some distance south of what was later known as the McCullah Settlement. A newer road that was later followed by the Butterfield Overland Mail and the Telegraph road continued south. The earlier road made a wide bow and joined the newer markings again on property that was later owned by the King-Ellis family. Few people of today remember hearing of the Springfield-Fayetteville road through Stone County.

In the left-hand corner of the map note that one John Allen was farming by row crops on both sides of Crane Creek at this time. This property is now owned by the Wire Road Wildlife Area, Missouri Conservation Commission.

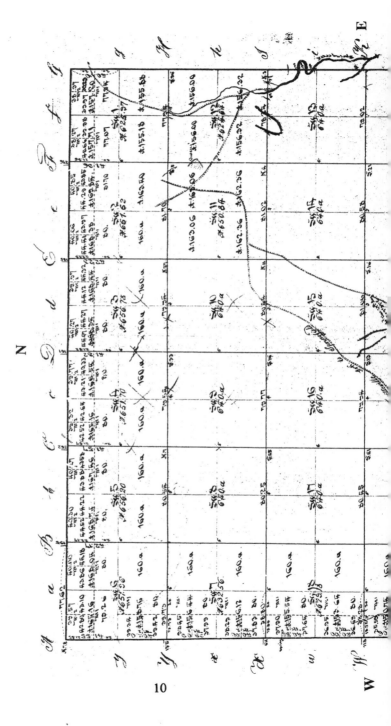

Township 26 North of the base line. Range 24 West of the 5th principal Meridian.

10

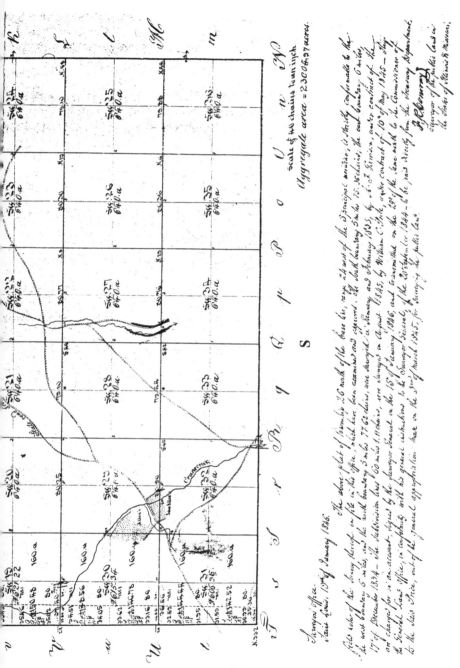

11

This house, known locally as the old Greene Peters home place is now owned and occupied by the Roger Roy family. The building, sturdy and strong, has stood on the old Wire Road for many years. The older Peters children recall their father hitching his horses to a wagon filled with wooden rain barrels. He then traveled several miles down the Wire Road to McCullah, or Chapel Springs, where he filled the barrels and returned home with water to supply the large family.

A unique fact about the house is that it faced the Wire Road which ran at an angle past the dwelling and so does not squarely face the roadway of today. The building is located near Brown's Spring, Missouri.

Chapter Two

The Battle of Wilson's Creek

View of Bloody Ridge, Wilson's Creek Battlefield National Park

The Battle of Wilson's Creek

The Wire Road played an important part in the decisive Battle of Wilson's Creek. The road crossed Wilson's Creek one-half mile north of Skeggs Branch, ten miles southwest of Springfield. This crossing is now within the boundaries of Wilson's Creek National Battlefield Park.

During the Civil War armies poured into the Missouri Ozarks from all directions, sometimes retreating along the same route. This was especially true before and after the Battle of Wilson's Creek and the Battle of Pea Ridge in Arkansas. The Wire or Telegraph Road followed the Butterfield Overland Mail route through Christian, Stone, and Barry counties. It is doubtful that the old Springfield-Fayetteville road which the Cherokee traveled was used to any great extent, especially through Stone County. Free-flowing springs were located at both the Alexander McCullah Settlement and at the Wesley McCullah Stop some three miles down the valley on the newer road.

The Men Who Commanded the Armies at the
Battle of Wilson's Creek.

Confederate Leaders:
Benjamin McCullough
Sterling Price
Nicholas Bartlett Pearce

Union Leaders:
Nathaniel Lyon
Frances Sigel
Samuel Sturgis

Benjamin McCulloch

Benjamin McCulloch commanded the Confederate forces at Wilson's Creek. Though possessing no formal military training, he was a veteran Indian fighter, participated in the Texas War of Independence and commanded a company of Texas Rangers in the Mexican War. After serving as sheriff of Sacramento during the California gold rush, he was appointed U.S. marshal for the eastern district of Texas. McCulloch rose from a colonel of State troops in February, 1861, to a brigadier general in the Confederate States Army in May of the same year. Seven months after the Confederate victory at Wilson's Creek, he died while leading a division of troops at the Battle of Pea Ridge, Arkansas, March 7, 1862.

Benjamin McCulloch

15

Sterling Price

Major General Sterling Price commanded the Missouri State Guard at Wilson's Creek. He had served in the Mexican War, the U.S. Congress, and as governor of Missouri. He accepted the command of the State Guard when the war began. At age 51, he was the oldest of the six principal commanders at Wilson's Creek and was well liked by his troops who affectionately nicknamed him, "Old Pap."

Sterling Price

Nicholas Bartlett Pearce

Nicholas Bartlett Pearce graduated from West Point in 1850 and served on the frontier for eight years before resigning from the Army. When Arkansas seceded in early 1861, its Confederate government commissioned him a brigadier general in charge of volunteers. At the Battle of Wilson's Creek, he commanded all Arkansas State troops.

Nicholas Bartlett Pearce

Nathaniel Lyon

Brigadier General Nathaniel Lyon, who commanded the Federal forces at Wilson's Creek, was an 1841 graduate of the U. S. Military Academy and a veteran of the Seminole and Mexican Wars. He had also served at various posts on the frontier before being assigned to command the U. S. arsenal in St. Louis in 1861. An ardent Unionist and a strong supporter of Lincoln and the Republican party, Lyon worked closely with Missouri Congressman Francis P. Blair, Jr., to prevent the state from seceding from the Union. His death at Wilson's Creek, at the age of 43 years, made him the first Union General to die in battle during the Civil War.

Nathaniel Lyon

Francis Sigel

German-born Franz Sigel was director of public schools in St. Louis at the onset of the Civil War. As colonel of the 3rd. Missouri Infantry, he took part in the capture of Camp Jackson in May, 1861, and fought in the Battle of Carthage two months later. The defeat of his 2nd. Missouri Brigade at Wilson's Creek helped forge the Southern victory.

Francis Sigel

Samuel Sturgis

Major Samuel Sturgis, who assumed command of the Union forces after Lyon's death, was an 1846 graduate of West Point. Like Lyon, he had served in the Mexican War and on the frontier. When the Civil War began, Sturgis was in command of the U. S. Army post at Ft. Smith, Arkansas. Cited for meritorious service at Wilson's Creek and in later battles, he rose to major general by war's end.

Samuel Sturgis

Skirmishes At Dug Springs and Curran

Brigadier General Nathaniel Lyon arrived in Greene County, Missouri in July, 1861. Shortly after Lyon's arrival in Springfield he was advised by scouts and spies that Major General Sterling Price and General Benjamin McCulloch, both of whom were in command of Confederate troops, were marching toward that city. General Lyon decided to move southward down the Wire Road to meet them.

Old spring house at Dug Springs

A short distance west of the small hamlet of Clever, Missouri, Lyon made contact with the enemy. On August 2, 1861, a skirmish took place at Dug Spring in Christian County. Losses were light on both sides with the Federals reporting five men killed and thirty-six wounded. The Confederates lost one officer and had five men wounded.

Hand-dug wells were common in the early days. Although Dug Spring was originally planned as a well, an abundance of water resulted in the decision to rock the walls of the opening and build a spring house. Dug Spring later became known as Hodge Spring, taking the name of a family who owned the property which surrounded the spring for many years. The spring which provided ample water for two armies still flows today.

On August 3, 1861, following the encounter at Dug Spring, General Lyon moved on southward to the Curran Post Office at the Alexander McCullah settlement, a short distance west of Brown's Spring. Reaching Curran, General Lyon discovered that a small Confederate patrol from Marionville had already arrived there. Preparing to eat their evening meal, they were surprised by shots from Lyon's Army. The soldiers scattered quickly and Lyon ordered his men to set up camp.

The 2d Kansas moved on down the valley some three miles to the Wesley McCullah Stop. The broad valley to the south of the trading post afforded this army an excellent camping place. Marking time at the McCullah Stop, the Federal forces were unaware that the Confederates were marshaling a sizable army at a point some three miles farther to the southwest where the Wire Road crossed Crane Creek.

General Lyon's army remained camped at Curran, or the McCullah Settlement, until word was received that the Confederates planned to cut off their return to Springfield. Lyon then decided to take his troops back to that city, a distance of twenty-four miles. The journey required two full days of travel. The army camped overnight on August 4, 1861, at Moody Springs on Terrell Creek.

The days following the skirmishes at Dug Spring and Curran were a time of great anxiety for people living along the Wire Road. With rumors afloat that a major battle was to be fought between the Union and Confederate forces in the immediate vicinity at any time, with thousands of soldiers already in the area, many families packed their possessions and sought safety elsewhere. Food was scarce but fields of green corn ripened in the summer sun; these were stripped bare by the hungry armies. Wagons were loaded with the grain, leaving farmers nothing to feed their starving livestock in the cold winter months ahead.

The Battle of Wilson's Creek, called Oak Hill by the

Confederates, was named for the stream where the battle took place. It was a bitter struggle between Union and Confederate forces for the control of Missouri in the first year of the Civil War. The fierce and bloody battle, lasting less than six hours, resulted in heavy causalities for both Federal and Confederate forces. The devastating hand to hand contact left many wounded men to die upon the battlefield; small wonder that the waters of Wilson's Creek ran red with the blood of men and horses.

General Nathaniel Lyon was wounded in the head and leg while leading his Federal troops at a place later called "bloody Hill". At 9:30 a. m. he was fatally wounded while urging his troops onward. Major Samuel Sturgis then assumed command of the Union Army. Realizing that the store of ammunition was nearly exhausted, he ordered a withdrawal to Springfield.

Losses were heavy, but they were about equal on both sides. The Federals lost 1,317 officers and men of the 5,400 engaged in battle. Number of the fatally wounded was 258, wounded 873, and missing 186. The Confederates lost 1,230 having 279 killed and 951 wounded of the 10,200 engaged in battle.

One hundred thirty years after cannons roared and men lay mortally wounded on the battlefield, Wilson's Creek flows lazily along at Wilson's Creek National Battlefield Park. A large number of visitors tour the grounds daily; perhaps they stop for a brief moment to remember the brave men who sacrificed their lives fighting for a principal they had sworn to uphold.

Wilson's Creek National Park

On April 26, 1987, The Wilson's Creek National Battlefield Park dedicated a new tour road that provides a driving tour of the park. The 4-8 mile road has been in use since September, 1986. Circling the park, the 19 foot roadway is restricted to one way driving so visitors will not have to worry about approaching traffic. Information and parking is provided at points of interest. The right side of the road includes a six foot lane for hiking. Biking and jogging through the 1,740 acre park.

The park service restored the John Ray home, complete with furnishings of the period. The home and companion buildings date prior to the Battle of Wilson's Creek. The Wire Road passed directly by the Ray home. The battle was a National re-enactment event in the summer of 2000.

The Wilson Creek Library, located next to the Visitors Center, is the largest Civil War library west of the Mississippi River and the second largest in the nation. The National Battlefield Park celebrated its one hundred-thirtieth anniversary in 1991.

Visitors Center at Wilson's Creek National Battlefield

The Battle of Madry

An encounter, sometimes referred to as the Battle of Madry, or the Battle of Upshaws farm, was fought in Barry County on October 29, 1864. The skirmish took place near the Wire Road, seven miles south of Verona, Missouri. The location was also near Camp Bliss.

Troops involved were thought to have been a part of those commanded by Sterling Price, Confederate leader. Federal troops were stationed near Verona at the time. It is possible that they encountered Confederate troops who were making their way southward to their homes.

After lasting only an hour all of the Confederate troops had been killed. The dead were loaded into an ox cart and were hauled to an old well where the bodies were dumped in a mass grave. After searching for three days for other casualties the well was then partially filled with dirt, and so became the final resting place of at least fourteen men.

Soldiers dumped in well in Barry County.

Cassville Republican November 6, 1899 listed an article about an old well which Ezekiel Ellis points out on his farm 7 miles south of Verona. He is son of Ben Ellis, living at the head of Little Flat Creek. His farm adjourns that of William Haynes on the east. Event occurred here after Battle of Wilson Creek (August 10, 1861). General Price made raid through Southern Missouri at Pilot Knob, was defeated and retreated into Kansas. Their army became partly disorganized and troops undertook to make way to home in Arkansas. A company of about 75 men, well armed and well mounted, passed near Verona. The date of the battle of Little Flat Creek tallies nearly exactly with the killing of the editor's grandmother north of Mt. Vernon. (Tombstone reads October 1862). She was wife of Hardin Davis, a brother of Elder Riley Davis. Sometime in the night, Price's men called at the gate and she rose and opened it. They, thinking it was the man of the house and having heard that he was a Union sympathizer, fired at the door, killing her instantly. They hurriedly rode away. Two days after a company corresponding to this rode down a little hollow that led to Little Flat Creek. The Union soldiers formed an ambuscade and after one-half hour clash had killed all the Confederates.

Zeke Ellis was then six years old and witnessed fight from a high hill on which his house now stands. He helped his father, mother and brother move dead by ox wagon to the above mentioned well. They dumped them in and after three days search for more bodies the well was partially filled up and now it is in the field, an unmarked resting place for a whole company of men who believed themselves fighting for a principle of right. (From Verona Advocate) (*I visited with several residents many years after this incident and they told me that their ancestors said these men had been in the area getting chickens, a day or two for their food supply. And one of the men was a black soldier. (When they were thrown into the well the last one landed on a post and was still visible the next day). The late Efton Thomas pointed the place out to Uncle Ralph Roden and me less than 1 mile from Clay Hill in which became Madry after the war.* twr

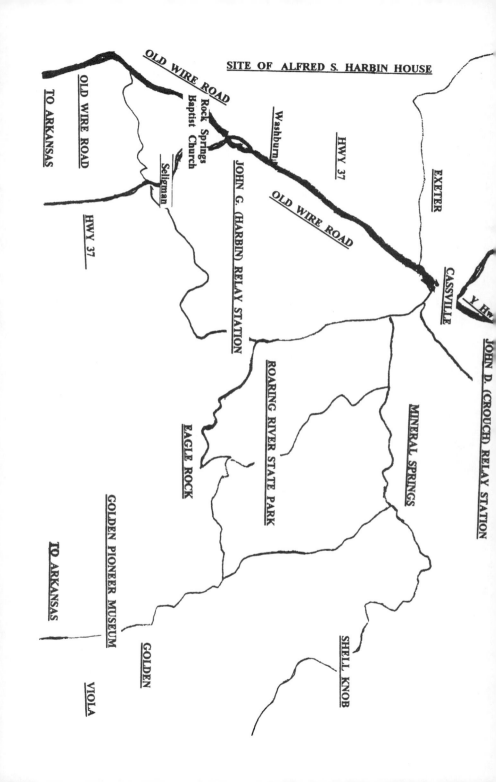

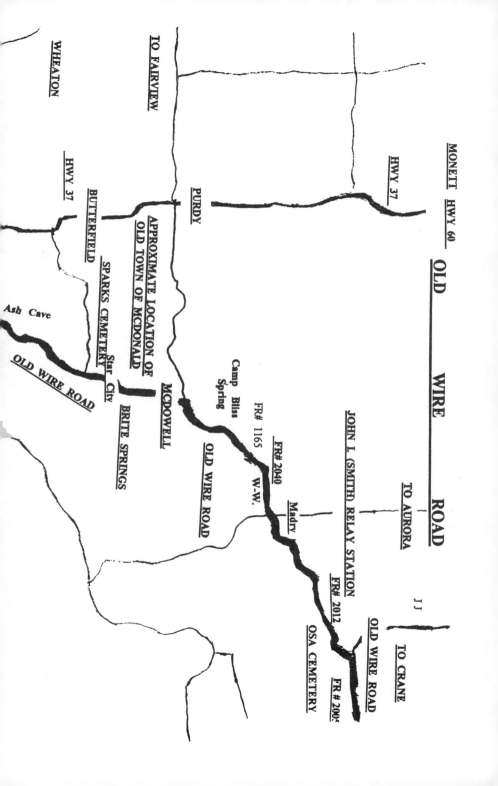

Official Actions of October 1864.

Oct. 28, 1864 - Engagement Newtonia MO 15th. Cavalry and AR 2nd. Calvary & others.
Oct. 29, 1864 - Skirmish Upshaw's farm
AR 2nd. Calvary
Oct. 29 - 30, " - Skirmishes Cane Creek (Crane)
MO 8th. State Militia
Oct. 30, " - Skirmish Newtonia
Springfield, Mo., October 31, 1864.

Major-General Rosecrans,

Warrensburg:

Lieutenant-Colonel Brutsche has just returned from a scout in Lawrence County, where he attacked a company of General Price's scouts, under Jenkins, and a battalion under Hodge. The rebels exhibited their usual panic and ran from inferior numbers. The enemy's loss is 100 killed and 133 prisoners. Our loss is 4 wounded and 4 horses. General McNeil's command is here shoeing and getting supplies. The enemy is devoting all his energies to the single point of getting away without any more fighting, and I think must succeed. He destroys no property, not even public. It required a march of ninety-two miles in thirty-six hours to force a battle the last time, and it will require more than that now. I have ordered all my serviceable cavalry and Boardman's battery to Cassville, and will move this column upon the enemy's trail at the earliest possible moment, although I do not anticipate striking the enemy. I shall move this column under command of Colonel Gravely, unless otherwise ordered by you. I am very decided in my judgment that the interests of the Government require that all the other cavalry should rest or be returned to Rolla by slow marches.

JOHN B. SANBORN,   *Brigadier-General, Commanding*

District of Southwest Missouri.

REPORT. 37.

Report of Lieutenant Hugh Cameron, Second Arkansas Cavalry (Union).

Headquarters Detachment.

In the Field, Mount Vernon, Mo., October 31, 1864.

General: I have the honor to report that on the 29th of October, 1864, with a detachment of about 400 men, principally of the Second Arkansas Calvary, I pursued a body of rebels, supposed to be 800 strong, under command of Colonel Hodge, from Buck Prarie, Lawrence County, and encountered them at the Upshaw farm near Camp Bliss, Barry County. Routed and dispersed them; killed 50, took 37 prisoners, 58 horses, 4 mules, a large number of saddles, and several stand of arms. Three wounded only were found; the remainder escaped on their horses or concealed themselves in the brush. The prisoners report that there were ten captains with Colonel Hodge, viz, Captains Thomas Todd and John Merrick, Captains Sitton, Kimball, Shull, Rudd, Withers, Onam, Arnold, and Anabury. The last named was killed early in the encounter. My loss was 1 slightly wounded, 1 man injured by his horse falling, and a few horses crippled.

The officers and men under my command behaved gallantly. Captain Mitchell, Seventh Provisional Enrolled Missouri, commanding the advance, deserves to be especially mentioned.

I have the honor to be, general, most respectfully, your obedient servant.

HUGH CAMERON,

Lieutenant-Colonel Second Ark. Cavalry,

Commanding Detachment in the field.

Brig. General John Sanborn, Commanding

Springfield, Mo., November 13, 1864

Colonel: I have the honor to submit the following report of the operations of my command during the late movement of the rebel army under General Price into and through the state.

Preparations for this campaign on the part of the rebels commenced in the valley of the White River about the 10th of June last, General Shelby arriving there with his division, seizing all mills and horses for the government use, and commencing a rigid conscription, as communicated in my telegraphic dispatches to department headquarters on the 15th and 16th of that month.

On the 29th of October Lieutenant-Colonel Cameron, Second Arkansas Cavalry, with a detachment of about 400 men, attacked a force of about 800 rebels in Barry County, and by a sudden dash broke the enemy's line killing 50 of his men, and capturing 37 men prisoners, 58 horses, 4 mules, some small arms, and other property. On the same day Lieutenant Colonel Brutsche attacked a body of rebels, killing a large number and taking a large number of prisoners.

Fortifications were constructed about Springfield and other posts in the district during the time the enemy was in the state.

The citizens and enrolled militia are entitled to great credit for their zeal and labors in driving the common enemy from the State and preserving this section of the state from devastation and ruin. These forces with the U.S troops remaining in the district have captured more than 800 prisoners, and otherwise greatly crippled the enemy. I have the honor to be, very respectfully, your obedient servant,

JOHN B. SANBORN, *Brigadier-General, Commanding,*

Col. John V. Du Bois, **Chief** *of Staff*

Chapter Three

The Trail Of Tears

1838-1839

NUNAHI - DUNA - DLO - HILU - I:
Trail Where They Cried

The Trail of Tears

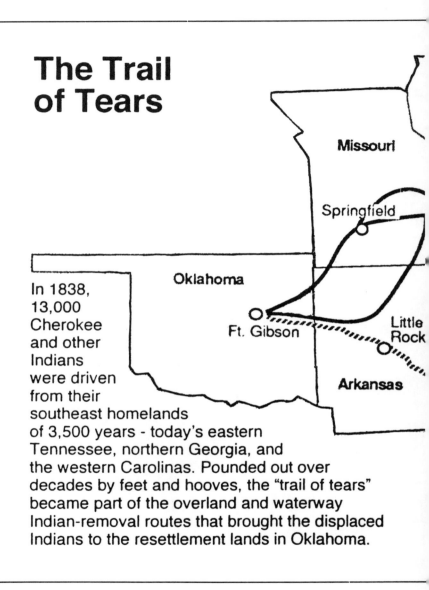

In 1838, 13,000 Cherokee and other Indians were driven from their southeast homelands of 3,500 years - today's eastern Tennessee, northern Georgia, and the western Carolinas. Pounded out over decades by feet and hooves, the "trail of tears" became part of the overland and waterway Indian-removal routes that brought the displaced Indians to the resettlement lands in Oklahoma.

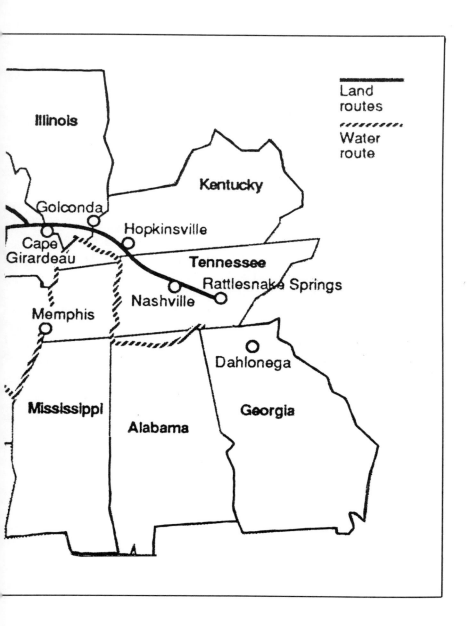

Land
routes

Water
route

Illinois

Kentucky

Golconda

Hopkinsville

Cape
Girardeau

Tennessee

Rattlesnake Springs

Nashville

Memphis

Dahlonega

Mississippi

Georgia

Alabama

The Trail Of Tears
1838 - 1839

Over one hundred fifty years have elapsed since thousands of Cherokee Indians passed through the Missouri Ozarks on their 800 mile journey to Oklahoma Territory, or The Cherokee Nation, West.

The forced removal of the Cherokee from their homes in the states of Alabama, Georgia, North Carolina, Tennessee, and Kentucky was a tragic happening. Herded into stockades like cattle, many died from exposure and disease before the actual march began. The long move westward resulted in death for one-fourth of the Cherokee Nation, and later became known as The Trail Of Tears. The Cherokee called it, "The trail where we cried."

This chapter deals with the reasons for, and methods of implementing the exodus. A later chapter contains authentic hand-written diaries of three conductors on parts of the trail which later became known as the Wire Road.

The State of Missouri had become known for its established roads. There is no doubt that this factor influenced the decision of Indian Conductor B. B.. Cannon, and other conductors to lead an approximate 12,000 Cherokee on the long trek westward, rather than choosing a shorter water route through Arkansas. The first detachment of Cherokee who moved westward of their own accord had chosen the water route. This group found that they were forced to make their way through swamp lands, losing many lives.

The Cherokee, a branch of the Iroquois Indians, were living in the southern states of North Carolina, Kentucky, Tennessee, Alabama, and South Carolina when ordered by General Winfield Scott on May 23, 1838, to sell their lands and move west to Oklahoma Territory.

As early as 1790, President Washington in a message to the Senate said, "During the last year I laid before the Senate a particular statement of the case of the Cherokee. By reference to that paper it will appear that the United States formed a treaty with the Cherokee in November, 1785; that the Cherokee thereby placed themselves under the protection of the United States and had a

34

boundary assigned them; that the white people who settled on the frontiers had openly violated said boundaries by intruding on Indian lands; that the United States assembled in Congress did on the last day of September, 1788, issue their proclamation forbidding all such warrantable intrusions and enjoined all those who had settled upon the hunting grounds of the Cherokee to depart with their families and effects without loss of time or they would answer their disobediences to the injunction and prohibitions expressed at their peril." Still the white people continued to trespass and encroach on the Indian lands, and new treaties were entered into from time to time. On January 17, 1798, President Adams appointed a commission to meet with the Cherokee. This treaty was signed October 2, 1798.

Differences arose within the Cherokee Nation. President Jefferson held a conference with representatives of the Upper Town and those of the Lower Town. Citizens of the Upper Town desired to live a civilized life and engage in agriculture on the lands occupied at that time. Those of the Lower Town did not desire to do this and asked that the reservation be divided giving land north of the Hiwassee River to the Upper Town, allowing them to form a government and adopt their own laws. Those of the Lower Town were willing to exchange their portion for land west of the Mississippi River as they desired to continue their own customs and habits of living. Since the wild game was fast disappearing, they desired to locate to new hunting grounds where game was more plentiful.

After hearing them, President Jefferson, desiring to be just, said all those who desired to remain where they then lived would be protected and assisted in the administration of their affairs, and all those dissatisfied with their surroundings might seek a location west of the Mississippi River along the reaches of the White and Arkansas rivers. Those who wished to leave met with General Jackson and other commissioners on July 8, 1817, and entered into a treaty to exchange their holdings in the east for a like territory west of the Mississippi. This migration to northwest Arkansas was a peaceful, planned movement approved by the government. Those who were left in the eastern states were a civilized people. They engaged in agriculture, the more wealthy owned slaves and some were better off financially than the large plantation owners of the south.

In 1821, Sequoyah, also known as George Gist, or Guess, devised a Cherokee alphabet. Sequoyah never went to school; he could neither read, write, or speak the English language. He was a hunter, trader, and a crafter of silverware. At one time he became disabled; it was then that he began to ponder on the fact that the white man could talk on paper. So he set to work; after twelve years he had perfected a system that stood for sounds in the language that proved easy to learn, the Cherokee alphabet contained 86 symbols. In 1828, a newspaper, the *Cherokee Phoenix*, was established and published regularly until it was silenced by Georgia authorities some ten years later. Sequoyah's translation of the Bible is proof that the Christian faith was embraced by the Cherokee nation.

In 1824, President Monroe, under the increasing pressure of the state of Georgia, and other southern states, requested the Cherokee to sell their land and move west of the Mississippi River. The Cherokee refused saying, "All men are created equal, they are endowed by their Creator with certain inalienable rights, among these are life, liberty, and the pursuit of happiness." At this time President Monroe expressed his belief that the Cherokee could only be moved by force.

The Cherokee population was near 15,000 in 1829. The tribe owned 22,000 cattle, 1,300 slaves, 2,000 spinning wheels, 700 looms, 31 grist mills, 10 saw mills, 8 cotton gins, and had 18 schools and a newspaper.

President Jackson, in 1829, declared in part, "My conclusion is that there cannot exist an independent government inside any state. I have so advised the Cherokee that they submit to the laws of the state or move beyond the Mississippi River." At the height of the Cherokee prosperity, gold was discovered near the present Dahlonega, Georgia, within the boundaries of the Cherokee nation. The greed of the white man fueled the fires, already burning, to have the Cherokee expelled from their Georgia homelands. Although the government had sworn to uphold the Cherokee rights, the New Echota, Georgia, removal treaty was signed on December 29, 1835.

Major Ridge, Cherokee leader, wrote President Andrew

Jackson saying, "We come now to address you on the subject of our griefs and afflictions from the acts of the white people. They have got our lands, and now they are preparing to fleece us of the money accruing from the treaty. We found our plantations taken either in whole, or in part, by the Georgians—suits instigated against us for back rent from our own farms. These suits are commenced in the inferior courts, with the evident design that when we are ready to remove, to arrest our people, and on these vile claims to induce us to compromise for our own release, to travel with our families. Thus our funds will be filched from our people, and we shall be compelled to leave our country as beggars and in want.

"Even the Georgia laws, which deny us our oaths, are thrown aside, and notwithstanding the cries of our people, and protestations of our innocence and peace, the lower classes of the white people are flogging the Cherokee with cow hides, hickories, and clubs. We are not safe in our houses; our people are assailed by day and by night by the rabble. Even justices of the peace and constables are concerned in this business. This barbarous treatment is not confined to men, but women are stripped also and whipped without law or mercy. Send regular troops to protect us from these lawless assaults and to protect our people as they depart for the West. If it is not done, we shall carry off nothing but the scars of the lash on our backs, and our oppressors will get all the money. We talk plainly, as chiefs having property and life in danger, we appeal to you for protection."

In spite of the pleas of the leaders of the Cherokee Nation, on May 23, 1838, General Winfield Scott ordered the removal of the Cherokee by force. By June he reported that nearly all had been taken prisoner. Some escaped into the hills of North Carolina where their descendants live today, but close to 15,000 were placed in concentration camps at Gunter's Landing, Alabama, on the Tennessee River; Old Town, Tennessee, near the Hiwassee River; Chattanooga, Tennessee; and Rattle Springs, Tennessee, near Charleston. Parties seized men working in the fields, women in their homes, and children at play, forcing them at the point of the bayonet to march away, taking them to stockades prepared where they were kept until ready to be moved. Conditions in the camps were deplorable, thousands died of starvation and exposure. At one time an epidemic of cholera ravaged the prisoners.

One party had already immigrated peacefully, the second party, supervised by Conductor B. B. Cannon, left in 1837. This detachment of 365 Cherokee was not a part of the Forced Removal but they were thought to have been the first group to travel through the Missouri Ozarks. Eleven more groups are said to have followed the B. B.. Cannon route through southwest Missouri and Arkansas Territory, and on to Indian Territory, near Ft. Gibson, Oklahoma Territory.

The B. B. Cannon diary tells of the illness, death, and heartache suffered by the Cherokee Nation on the Trail of Tears. The removal will be remembered as one of the most glaring examples of man's inhumanity to man. One doctor stated that at least 2,000 of the 15,000 who migrated had died by December 26, 1838, and that as many as one-fourth of the Cherokee Nation died eventually as a result of the march.

The average cost per party was between $65,000 and $75,000. A conductor, physician, wagoner, and interpreter were all paid by the United States government. Subsistence pay of .16c per person, per day was allotted for food. Only one wagon was furnished for 20 persons and one horse per five persons. Some of the larger groups had as many as 60 wagons, 600 horses, 80 oxen, and 1,000 Cherokee. Many walked most of the long journey, only the elderly and children could ride.

Many of the young Cherokee men hunted along the trail. In accordance with the Cherokee custom any game killed in the forest was left for the women to bring to camp, dress and cook. As the hunters returned to camp twigs were broken to guide them to the site of the kill. With salt pork issued almost daily, the fresh meat was a welcome addition to the meals.

"...And Then He Heard A Baby Cry."

The following true story related to Evert Lee Hair, Sr., by his father and grandfather happened near the small town of Boaz, Missouri. The Cherokee on the ill-fated Trail of Tears were known to have camped near the site of Delaware Town on the James River, only a short distance from the Boaz settlement.

It was a cold, dreary December day in the Missouri Ozarks, the dead of winter. A slight skiff of snow had fallen throughout the day. The old Indian Trail which ran near the Hair home was deserted. Travelers were few and far between in the rough, hilly country, especially so in winter months. Gray clouds hung low over the hills and valleys, a good sign of still another blast of winter weather to come. Along the old trail, and in sparsely settled communities, farmers were busily scattering hay to bed down the livestock for the long winter night. Wood carried inside was stacked high to feed the open fireplaces.

A short distance from the Hair home, a detachment of Cherokee Indians, victims of the forced exodus from Georgia, Tennessee, and North Carolina, to the Oklahoma Territory, were preparing to make camp for the night. The glow of large bonfires, built for heat and cooking, lit up the countryside for miles around with their fingers of flame. Sadly enough, the glowing fires did but little to ease the discomfort of the cold, sickness, and suffering in the camp. Many had died since the march had begun; burials were held daily. Mothers whose children had died along the march carried them in their arms until the group halted for the night.

The following morning dawned, clear and cold. The conductor, perhaps ever mindful of the deteriorating condition of his charges, lost no time in breaking camp and urging his followers onward. A neighbor of the Hair family, concerned about the condition of the grounds where the Indians had camped the night before, decided to investigate. Nearing the campsite he was startled by a noise—and then he heard a baby cry. Hurrying to the site, he found a newborn baby girl wrapped in a blanket under some leaves and placed near a tree. It was obvious that the tiny, newborn child had been abandoned by its Cherokee mother. Perhaps she knew that it could not survive the hardships of the remainder of the journey, so she took a chance that it might be found.

The neighbor gathered the baby girl in his arms and headed home to tell his wife of his find. The couple had no children, so they took the infant to their hearts and loved her as if she were their own. She was named Annie and later in life became known as

Indian Annie. Annie was married to a Negro boy, the son of a slave belonging to a brother of the man who found her. When the young couple were married, the foster parents deeded them forty acres of their best farming land. Living near the small town of Boaz, they reared a family of five children, two sons and three daughters. The sons moved to Kansas City, and the daughters settled in Springfield.

The Frazier Chapel was a short distance from Boaz; Annie and her family attended church there. In the olden days many people rode horses to church, tying them to trees while the services were in progress. This family owned and rode the best horses in the community. Their saddles were of the finest quality of leather with gleaming, silver ornaments.

Although Evert Hair was only a small boy, he remembered seeing Annie and her family. At that time he had known Annie's full name, but like so many other things it had been forgotten. He surmised that the family was probably buried in the Frazier Chapel Cemetery, or in the old Delaware Cemetery. Seeking information on the family several years ago he found no trace of anyone who remembered them.

In Tribute To The Cherokee

Slowly, but surely, steps are being taken to recognize the dreadful ordeal that the Cherokee suffered on the Trail of Tears. Our history books have been woefully lacking in describing the Forced Indian Removal and the shame and injustice endured as a result of this action.

In December, 1987, Congress recognized the story of the Cherokee relocation as a significant part of American history and designated the Trail of Tears as a National Historic Trail. The National Park Service is now preparing a comprehensive management plan for the Trail of Tears Historic Trail. The plan will provide guidance for managing the trail and telling an accurate story of the Cherokee's tragic experience.

The proposed trail will begin at New Echota, Georgia, and at Ft. Butler, North Carolina. Both routes will end at Tahlequah, Oklahoma, the capitol of the western Cherokee. In Missouri the trail will follow state and federal highways from Cape Girardeau, home of the Trail of Tears State Park. It will go through Farmington and Potosi to Rolla, then southwest along Interstate I-44 through Lebanon and Springfield. From there U.S. 60 will carry the trail to Monett, and down highway 37 into Arkansas.

The trail will cost an estimated $220,000, (no property will be acquired) and will consist of markers on existing highways closest to the trail or river.

The trail will be a living history, geography, and social science lesson to students in the two-hundredth year of our Constitution that not all confrontations between branches of government were settled constitutionally to our shame and the innocent deaths of many. Richard L. Paugh, business manager for the Eastern Cherokee Nation Overhill Band, said: "The trail is the first step in atonement to a proud nation that existed for over 5,000 years on this continent."

Wagon Train Traces Trail Of Tears - 1988

In early October, 1988, a wagon train of horses and horse-drawn vehicles left Cleveland, Tennessee, on a journey to commemorate the one hundred-fiftieth Anniversary of the Trail of Tears. Averaging an approximate twenty miles per day the group reached Tahlequah, Oklahoma, the final stop for those on the original trail, on December third, 1988. The project was organized by representatives of the states through which the forced march passed in 1838-1839. These states were: Tennessee, Kentucky, Illinois, Missouri, Arkansas, and Oklahoma.

Tom Gulley, Marion, Illinois, was Wagon Master. Gulley and his wife Cheryl, were married in a barn in Woodbury, Tennessee, shortly after the journey began. A. J. "Curly" Weil, Grayville, Illinois, drove the second wagon. Weil's wagon, as well as several others, was equipped for all kinds of weather with a small electric generator and a propane heater.

The actual Trail of Tears crossed the Christian-Stone County line some five miles due east of Marionville, and then followed a southwest direction through Stone and Barry counties. The trail did not enter Lawrence County as did the commemorative train in 1988, the wagon train followed established routes nearest the old trail.

The Cherokee Wagon Train arrived in Marionville, Missouri, in a cold, driving rainstorm on November 26, 1988. After the horses had been cared for and all preparations for the night had been made, the travelers were treated to a hot meal of vegetable soup, chili, corn bread, pie, and cake. Several pots of steaming hot coffee around a glowing campfire, live music, and an interesting program ended the festivities.

Wagons roll out of Marionville on Sunday, Nov. 20, after an early snowstorm the night before.

Sunday morning dawned with a surprising two inches of snowfall. The cold, wintry weather was a grim reminder of the trials of the Cherokee during the forced Indian Removal. Wagon Master, Tom Gulley, calmly reminded those who followed him that there is only one thing to do during inclement weather—"pull your hat down over your eyes—and keep going."

43

Tom Gulley says, "If the weather is bad, pull your hat down and keep going."

Leaving Marionville—next stop Monett, Mo.

44

Trail of Tears State Park

Jackson, Missouri

Photograph by Haupt Studio, Jackson, Mo.

THE SHRINE TO PRINCESS OTAHKI

Otahki is a legendary princess, and this shrine located in this State Park is a memorial to the many who died on this dreadful winter journey 1838-39.

The third detachment of 950 Cherokees started westward in late '38 and crossed the Mississippi river filled with floating ice in the bitter cold of December. Many were ill; the exposure and hardship was too much. Among those who died and were buried here by the wayside was Princess Otahki.

Much of the story about Princess Otahki, once accepted as fact, has now been disproved, but the misfortune, hardships and deaths suffered by these Indians is told so well in this story and did occur similarly to hundreds, that it deserves to live on as legend.

A fitting tribute to the Cherokee is the State Park in Cape Girardeau, Missouri. From Jackson, Missouri, the park may be reached by following the Green's Ferry Road which is, for the most part, the trail over which the Cherokee came.

This State Park, consisting of 3,346 acres was a gift to the State of Missouri by the residents of Cape Girardeau County, and contains a portion of the route used by the Cherokee on the march from Georgia, Alabama, and Tennessee to Oklahoma.

A dense and healthy stand of trees covers the area which includes many fine specimens of American beech, tulip, winged elm, Spanish oak, and dogwood. The trailer park has facilities for water, electricity, and disposal. The Shrine to Princess Otahki is located in the State Park.

Blue Springs

One route that the Cherokee followed on the Trail of Tears led them through northern Arkansas. At Blue Springs, seven miles west of Eureka Springs, the old roadbed is still visible. Located in a beautiful park, Blue Springs has a capacity of thirty-eight million gallons of water every twenty-four hours. Blue in color, the water is reported to be of glacier origin flowing from the Pacific northwest via an underground river. Temperature of the water remains at 54 degrees Fahrenheit winter and summer.

De Soto's party visited the spring in 1541, and the French in 1686 and 1773. In 1804, ex-governor Boggs and Daniel Boone camped at the spring for several days and secured a guide to take them to Cane Hill, Arkansas. They again stopped on their journey home the following spring.

The Cherokee camped at Blue Springs for several days before resuming their journey. A large hieroglyphic rock bears witness to the many Indians who lived in the area.

Ancient Cherokee Lore

A long time ago there was no earth, nothing but water. Above,

46

beyond the solid stone arch of the sky, was a world where dwelt all the animals. In time it became crowded up there, and the animals began to look about for a new home.

They gazed down at the vast water of this lower world and wondered what was below it. Finally, they sent Water Beetle, grandchild of Beaver, to look around. Water Beetle dove deep into the water and brought up a little piece of soft mud. Floating upon the water, this bit of mud began to spread and spread until it became the vast earth. It was flat and square, and later on someone, no one knows who, fastened it with long cords at each of its four corners to the sky.

The animals then sent down the Great Buzzard to reconnoiter. He found the earth all soft and wet, with no dry place to rest. He became very tired by the time he reached the Cherokee country, and his weary wings began to flap and flap, striking the wet ground. His tremendous wings would strike the earth, and there would be a valley; they would turn upward, and there would be a mountain. This is why the Cherokee country is so hilly.

The animals lived on the earth first, then a brother and sister came to found the human race. The man began to kill the animals and birds; when the trouble became so grave, the animals and birds held council together. They wished to avenge their wrongs, but at first they could think of no plan. Then the birds and the insects devised a number of diseases which they decided they would visit upon man.

But all the plants of the forest remained friendly to man, and so they agreed among themselves that they would furnish a cure for every disease the birds and insects might devise. This is why herbs have always furnished the most beneficial medicine.

> Screaming the night away
> With his great wing feathers
> Swooping the darkness up
> I hear the Eagle bird
> Pulling the blanket back
> off from the eastern sky.
>
> Iroquois poem

47

ARETHA
F.J.

Walini, the famous singer, a lovely maiden sang all along the
Trail of Tears to hearten her people. This is the song she sang:

Cherokee, warrior, hunters,
Children of the great Hiawatha,
Tho the snow of winter binds us
And the voices of the forest
Come unbidden to our campfire,
Still before us are the prairies,
Land of sunshine, not of darkness,
Homeland, where the streamlets murmur
Through the gorges of the mountains,
Where the bounding deer await us
And the feasts are spread before us,
Where the green corn smiles in beauty,
Tahlequah, Tahlequah.

Chapter Four

Diaries Of Conductors On The Trial

Of Tears

1837-1839

From the diary of B. B. Cannon:
Decr. 17, 1837 Snowed last night. Buried Ellegee's wife and
Charles Timberlake's son (Smoker)

Diaries Of Conductors On The Trail Of Tears

The following diaries are day to day accounts recorded by conductors Rev. Daniel S. Buttrick, B. B. Cannon, and Dr. W. I. I. Morrow as they guided the Cherokee on the Trail of Tears.

The overland route entered Springfield, Missouri, from the northeast, having followed the White River Trace from Green's Ferry, on the Mississippi River near Cape Girardeau, Missouri. This route was also known as the Ozark Indian Trace and it paralleled roughly the present Interstate I-44, from near St. Louis to Springfield.

The following is a statement from Jere Krakow, head historian of the National Park Service, Denver, Colorado: "We believe the route (Trail of Tears) differed from the Butterfield route south of Springfield, Missouri, going back across James River near the mouth of Wilson's Creek before swinging back west and south in Stone County, thereby joining the Butterfield. The basis of our maps in Missouri are the original land survey records at the Department of Natural Resources, Rolla, Missouri. We contracted with Duane King of the Museum of the American Indian to do the detailed mapping and site inventory component of the plan. Dr. King has been employed by both the Cherokee Nation and the Eastern Band of Cherokee over the years, and is fluent in Cherokee."

Quoting Fairbanks and Tuck, "The Bolivar or Booneville road followed the Osage Indian Trace. The early settlers knew this road as the "old road" or the "military road." It extended from Palmyra on the Mississippi River through Booneville, Springfield, Delaware Town and Fayetteville, Arkansas, to Ft. Smith. Beyond Springfield, it was sometimes known as the Delaware Trace. It was regularly located and cut out to the legal width in accordance with an order issued at the first term of the Greene County Court. This road was declared to be "a public highway in Greene County to the State line."

At its June 22, 1836 meeting the Greene County Court proceeded to lay off road districts of the State road passing through the county. District No. 1 was to extend from the courthouse in Springfield to Wilson's Creek, "on the State road in the direction of the Arkansas line, including all the settlements east of the old road and Delaware Town and south of the courthouse." William Dye was named overseer of this district. (Information Greene County court records. 1836. page 219.)

Thus for a number of years during the late 1830's and into the 1840's there were two roads leading southward from Springfield to the Arkansas line. The oldest of these, the Delaware Trace, led southward from Springfield and crossed the James River in Section 27, Township 28, Range 23, West. By 1861, few, if any, travelers enroute from Springfield to northwestern Arkansas would have taken the Delaware Trace. (*Fairbanks and Tuck, Past and Present of Greene County.*)

Louis Ross, Contractor of Subsistence claim against the Government Report

Name of Conductor	Number	Died	Born	Date Arrived
Elijah Hicks	729	57	9	1-14-1839
Harris Conrad	858	54	5	1-7-1839
Jesse Bushyhead	950	38	6	2-23-1839
John	1200	33	3	1-10-1839
Situakee	1250	71	5	5-22-1839
Stephen Forman	983	57	19	2-27-1839
Mose Daniels	1035	48	6	3-2-1839
Choo-Wa-Loo-ka	1150	no report		3-1-1839
Jessie Brown	850	34	3	3-5-1839
George Hicks	1118	no report		3-14-1839
Richard Taylor	1029	55	15	3-24-1839
Pete Hilderbrand	1766	no report		3-25-1839
John Ross	219	no report		2-1-1839

This is a total of 13,137 Cherokee Indians moved by 13 different detachments. Recorded deaths along the way totaled 447, births, 71. These figures do not include the four detachments which kept no records of deaths and births along the way.

We now have, on excellent authority, proof that the Butterfield Overland Mail route, and later the Telegraph Road, did not follow the Trail of Tears route through Christian County, Missouri. Merging near the Christian-Stone County line the three routes were one and the same for a short distance. See Springfield-Fayetteville map on pages 10 and 11. The National Park Service, Denver, Colorado, seeking to chart the route of the Cherokee through the Ozarks will use the Springfield-Fayetteville road as a part of the trail after extensive research.

The two routes, the Springfield-Fayetteville road which the Trail of Tears followed, and the so-called Wire Road which was used by the Butterfield Overland Mail route and later the Wire or Telegraph road, crossed Crane Creek at a location some one and one-half miles west of the present town of Crane, Missouri.

Rev. Daniel S. Buttrick Diary 1838

Detachment No. 11 - Richard Taylor
Assistant Conductor - Adair
Physician - Dr. W. I .I. Morrow
Wagonmaster - G. W. Parks

1,029 Cherokee

This detachment of 1,029 Cherokee left Brainerd (Presbyterian Mission School) on October 4, 1838. Space does not permit recording the entire diary here. This group was on the trail over five months, arriving in the Cherokee Nation, West, on March 25, 1838.

Thur. March 7 - Traveled to west branch of Gasconade.

Sat. March 9 - Traveled 18 miles to Mr. Burnett's still on Osage branch Gasconade.
Mon. March 11 - Traveled 12 miles, Mr. Hilderbrand on another road.
Tue. March 12 - **Camped on** beautiful prairie, camped at

52

sunset.

Wed. March 13 - Through some large prairie to Springfield.

Thur. March 14 - Traveled 8 miles, crossed stream called St. James.

Fri. March 15 - Traveled 17 miles over barren desert to stream Sugar Creek.

Sat. March 16 - 26 miles to a Mr. Mason's from Tennessee.

Mon. March 18 - Traveled 20 miles, rained

Tue. March 19 - Proceed about 9 miles in rain.

Wed. March 20 - Traveled 6 miles.

Thur. March 21 - and Fri. March 22 - traveled about 26 miles - eight miles from Nation.

Sat. March 23 - Proceeded 8 miles to Mr. Woodhall's place of deposit and where Mr. Taylor is to deliver the detachment over to U.S. States officer.

Sun. March 24 - Had meeting, considerable numbers of Cherokee attending.

Mon. March 25 - Made arrangements to send Jonas, the little boy who came with us, to his father, gave our tent to an old Cherokee woman who had none, and took our leave of the dear detachment with whom we had been wandering these past five months.

Author's Note:

It can be assumed that the Buttrick group spent the night of March 15, on Crane Creek, not Sugar Creek. They had spent the previous night on James River and had traveled 17 miles, the approximate distance from James River to Crane Creek.

Journal Of Occurances
B. B. Cannon

The following is a hand-written account from a diary kept by B. B. Cannon, Conductor on the Trail of Tears. Lack of space prevents copying the Journal in its entirety. The document is reprinted courtesy the National Archives, Special File 249.

On October 13, 1837 a detachment of 365 Cherokee Indians under the supervision of Conductor B. B. Cannon left the Cherokee Agency East to travel 800 miles to Ft. Gibson, Cherokee Indian Agency West. This account begins when the group had been on the Trail for two months and were nearing Springfield, Missouri.

Decr. 13, 1837   Marched at 8-1/2 o'clock A.M. halted at a branch near Mr. Ellingtons 4 o'clock P.M. encamped and issued corn and fodder. Reese and Mayfield camp - 13-1/2 miles today.

Decr. 14, 1837   Marched at 8 o'clock A. M. halted at James fork of White River near the road but which does not cross the road 3 o'c P.M. Mr. Wells taken sick. Issued corn meal, corn and fodder. 15-1/2 miles today.

Decr. 15, 1837   Joseph Starrs wife had a child last night Marched at 8 A. M. halted at Mr. Danforths 2 o'c P.M. waggoners having horses shod until late at night. encamped and issued corn fodder and beef 10 miles today.

Decr. 16, 1837   Issued sugar and coffee to the waggoners and interpeters this morning Marched at 9 o'c A.M. passed through Springfield, Mo. halted at Mr. Clicks 4 o'c P.M. encamped and issued corn and fodder and corn meal. 12 miles today (left Mr. Wells.)

Decr. 17, 1837   Snowed last night Buried Elleges wife and Charles Timberlake's son (Smoker) Marched at 9 o'c A.M. halted at Mr. Dye's at 3 o'c P.M. extremely cold weather, sickness prevailing to a considerable extent, all very much fatigued encamped and issued corn and fodder and beef, 10 miles today.

Decr. 18, 1837   Detained on account of sickness Doct. Townsend sent back to Springfield, for medicine. Buried Dreadful Waters this evening. Issued corn and fodder and corn meal.

Decr. 19, 1837   Detained today also on account of sickness, cold intense. Issued corn and fodder, and beef.

Decr. 20, 1837   Marched at 8 o'c A.M. halted at Mr. Allen's 1/2 past 3 o'c encamped and issued corn and fodder, and corn meal 15 miles today.

Decr. 21, 1837   Marched at 8 o'c A.M. halted at Locke's on Flat Creek 1/2 past 3 o'c P.M. encamped and issued corn and fodder, and corn meal, 15 miles today.

Decr. 22, 1837 Buried Goddard's grandchild Marched at 8 o'c A.M. halted at McMurtery 3 o'c P.M. encamped and issued corn and fodder, and corn meal. 15 miles today.

Dec. 23, 1837 Buried Rainfrog's daughter (Lucy Redstick's child) Marched at 8 o'c A.M. halted at Reddix 3 o'c P.M. encamped and issued corn and fodder and beef. 16 miles today.

Decr. 24, 1837 Marched at 8 o'c A.M. halted at the X hollows, had to leave the road 3/4 mile to get water 3 o'c P.M. Issued corn fodder, pork and cornmeal 15 miles today.

Decr. 25, 1837 Marched at 8 o'c A.M. took the right hand road to Cane Hill, at Fitzgeralds halted a half mile in advance of Mr. Cunningham's at a branch. 3 o'c P.M. Issued corn fodder and salt pork 15-1/2 miles today.

Decr. 26, 1837 Marched at 8 o'c A.M. halted at James Coulters on Cane Hill ar. 3 o'c P.M. issued corn and fodder, corn meal, encamped 16-1/2 miles today.

Decr. 27, 1837 Buried Alsey Timberlake, daughter of Charles Timberlake Marched at 8 o'c A.M. halted at Mr. Beams in the Cherokee Nation West at 1/2 past 2 o'c P.M. encamped and issued corn and fodder, fresh pork, and some beef. 12 miles today.

Decr. 28, 1837 The party refused to go further but at the same time pledged themselves to remain together until the remuster was made by the proper officer for who I immediately sent an express to Ft. Gibson, they alleged at the same time that the refusal was in consequence of the sickness now prevailing and that only Dr. Reynolds disbursing agent for the party dismissed the wagons from further service. Buried another child of Charles Timberlake's and one which was born (Untimely) yesterday of which no other account than this is taken. Jesse Half Breeds wife had a child last night. Issued pork, corn meal, and flour, corn and fodder today. Lieut. Van Thorne arrived late this evening having issued the express on the way.

Decr. 29, 1837 Remustered the party. Issued quanity of corn meal and pork.

Decr. 30, 1837 Completed the rolls of muster, turned over the party to Lieut. Van Thorne and dismissed my assistants.

Respectfully Submitted

B. B. Cannon Conductor

Diary of Dr. W. I. I. Morrow   1837

It is apparent that this detachment followed the northern overland route charted by Conductor B. B. Cannon. A lack of space prevents the reprinting of the diary in its entirety.

March 12 - Detachment started before day, traveled 12 miles to Dansforth's-warm day- turned cold during the night. Snowing in the morning.

March 13 - Cold morning. Came on to Springfield, 8 miles. Got no letter from home, much disappointed- Alfred Indian living here-Springfield is a rich country-many Indians got drunk.

March 14 - Fine morning, clear and calm.General Smith, tavern keeper a clever fellow. Travel to Dyer (Bell Tavern) 12 miles.

March 15 - Clear and fine morning, traveled 17 miles to Allen's, said to be good house. A waggon (sic) ran over a little Indian's head, had to go to camp to see him. Stayed in Camps the first time since I left Illinoise.

March 16 - Traveled 12 miles to Lock's in Barry County on Flat Creek, a branch of White River. Lock a gambler and hunter, did not sleep much. The girls and boys talked and laughed all night. A fine pleasant day.

March 17 - Sunday traveled up Flat Creek, 15 miles to McMurtres - eat dinner at Mason's 2 miles northeast of McMurtres - fine day.

March 18 - Clear and warm, traveled through Washburn's Prairie and to Pratt's 18 mile - crossed the line of Arkansas and Missouri near Meek's on Sugar Creek, 7 miles northeast of Pratt's. Monday night, hail, rain, wind, and thunder.

March 19, - Rain all day Did not travel.

March 20 - Cloudy and cool, traveled 15 miles to the X Hollows eat dinner at Homesly's and came on 5 miles to Fitzgerald's in company with Cox Fields, Hemgar, and Geo. D. Morrow - a mean house.

March 21 - Thursday-cloudy and cool - passed through Fayetteville and met the detachment at Cunningham's 3 miles from town - did not get a letter at town - much disappointed. Fayetteville in Washington County - fertile land around it - beautiful situation - a good courthouse - Bank house and some other good buildings got a mean dinner at the brick tavern. From Cunningham's, we traveled to Col. Thomason's on the 22 of March - 16 miles, and on Saturday 23, we arrived at Woodall's in the Cherokee Nation, West. 3 miles from the boundary line.

March 24 - Sunday, most of the Indians turned over to the government - settled my business and on Monday 25, left for John Ross headquarters - traveled down Barren Fork of Illinois and over to the main river and took lodging at Wm. Key's - Jim Brown there.

March 26 - Left after breakfast - saw C.N. Cowan - got $6.00 - arrived at Coaday's for dinner, 10 miles - got dinner and went down to Ft. Gibson, 10 miles - returned from Ft. Gibson to Mrs. Coaday's and stayed all night - saw Betty Cheek there.

March 27 - Came up to Coady's - tried to get my business settled, did not accomplish my object until Sunday, 1 o'clock when we (Brother George, I. I. Fields, and black George) started for home - and traveled to Smith's 18 miles.

April 1 - Left Smith's after breakfast - pd $1.50 - 12 miles to Mrs. Weber's - 8 miles to Vineyard - stopped at Wilson's - saw L. O. Taylor and Patterson. Got some good liquor, came down to Lea's Creek to Knox's - 16 miles from Vineyard - passed Devault at natural mill dam. Stopped at — — paid $1.50.

Author's note:

Dr. Morrow apparently did not return by the same route that the detachment of Cherokee followed on the way to the Cherokee Nation, West. Farther on, he makes mention of the towns of Little Rock, Arkansas, and Memphis, Tennessee, which would have been on the southern route. Dr. Morrow did not note the hardships, suffering, and death that Conductor B. B. Cannon recorded in his *Journal of Occurances*.

Dr. W. I. I. Morrow

Later information on Dr. W. I. I. Morrow reveals that under

military appointment as Major, acting in the capacity of surgeon, he went from Tennessee to the Indian Territory with a company of Indians—Cherokee, Seneca, etc., for their relocation.

In 1851, he came as agent to the Indians under appointment of President Millard Fillmore. At this time he brought his family consisting of his grandparents, Aunt Mary and two children, with Aunt Cilla coming in a barouche, driving two grey horses. Others rode in covered wagons, driving a spike team (three horses, one in front of the two), Uncle Will and George riding horseback. They also brought three dogs belonging to various members of the family. They started on the first of November and were two months on the road.

> Neosho Agency,
> October 1, 1852.
>
> Sir: In compliance with the regulations of the Indian department, I have the honor to submit the following report in relation to the affairs of my agency:
>
> The Senecas, ... Their proximity to the State of Missouri affords them all the facilities they desire to procure whiskey. A distillery has been in successful operation for a number of years at Enterprise, near the State line. It is now conducted by a Mr. Houghton, who furnishes not only the Senecas, but all other Indians who call upon him, any amount of whiskey they can pay for. He has been so long engaged in this traffic, and the laws of Missouri are so defective, that it is impossible to detect him, and visit him with such punishment as the nature of his offence merits. I regret to say that the principal chief of the Senecas is a very intemperate man, and is doing great injury to his people by his example.
> ...... I am, very respectfully, your obedient servant,
>
> C.P. John Drennen,
> Supt. Indian Affairs, Van Buren, Ark.   W. J. J. Morrow, U.S. Indian Agent

Letter written by W. I. I. Morrow, Indian Agent, Neosho, Missouri, to Col. John Drennon, Superintendant Indian Affairs, Van Buren, Arkansas, October 1, 1852.

The Trail or Thong Tree

Pictured is a thong tree which still grows near the location of the McCullah, or Chapel Spring, near Brown's Spring, Missouri. The trees, usually made of oak saplings, were tied down with a strip of leather or a piece of bark from another tree. The saddle, or bent section, of the small tree soon grew in a horizontal position and served to point the Indian travelers to "live" water. Water was a necessity and the term "live" denoted water which ran from a perpetual spring, or river, which flowed both winter and summer. Wild game also inhabited the areas where a souce of water could be found.

To shape the sapling the Indians first drove the base of one forked stick into the ground near the foot of the sapling. Then they placed the other forked stick upside down over the trunk, driving the two prongs in the ground.

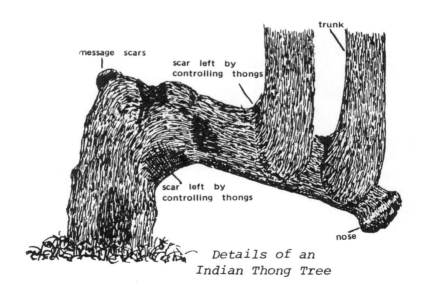

Details of an Indian Thong Tree

Chapter Five

The Butterfield Overland Mail

"Remember boys, nothing on God's green earth must stop the United States Mail."

The Overland Mail

61

The Butterfield Overland Mail
1859-1861

Some 20 years had elapsed since the last detachment of Cherokee had passed through the Missouri Ozarks. Rumors were being heard of a new company, the Butterfield Overland Mail, and hopes were high for regular mail delivery and transportation to this area and beyond.

The Butterfield Overland Mail was not, however, the first regularly scheduled mail route over the old road. On May 20, 1846, the Federal government had entered into a contract with Joseph Burdin, Springfield, to transport mail three times a week from Springfield to Fayetteville, Arkansas, in a two horse stage for the sum of $1,000 per year. It is not clear when this route was discontinued.

When word arrived that gold had been discovered in California, there was a demand for faster and better service to that state and the west coast. Congressman John S. Phelps, Missouri, and Senator William M. Gwinn, California, ever mindful of the wishes of their constituents later introduced a bill that was to establish the first cross-country mail service. This bill was passed on March 3, 1857. The Postmaster General was authorized to issue a contract to that effect.

The bill specified that service was to begin within a year after the contract was awarded. It also stated that four good horses, coaches, or spring wagons were to be used and trips were to be made in 25 days. The bids were opened in June, 1857.

The contract was awarded to John Butterfield, Utica, New York. The 2,800 mile route began in Tipton, Missouri, the end of the railroad from St. Louis, Missouri, and ran to San Francisco, California. The firm purchased 1,200 horses, 600 mules, over 250 regular coaches, special mail wagons, and water tanks. Existing farmers along the route were often designated as station managers, and their farm as a regular scheduled mail collection point. The wives of the station managers also earned a most welcome added income serving meals to the drivers and passengers. Over 1,000 local farmers were hired as blacksmiths, conductors, drivers, and veterinarians. The horses had to be groomed and ready when the

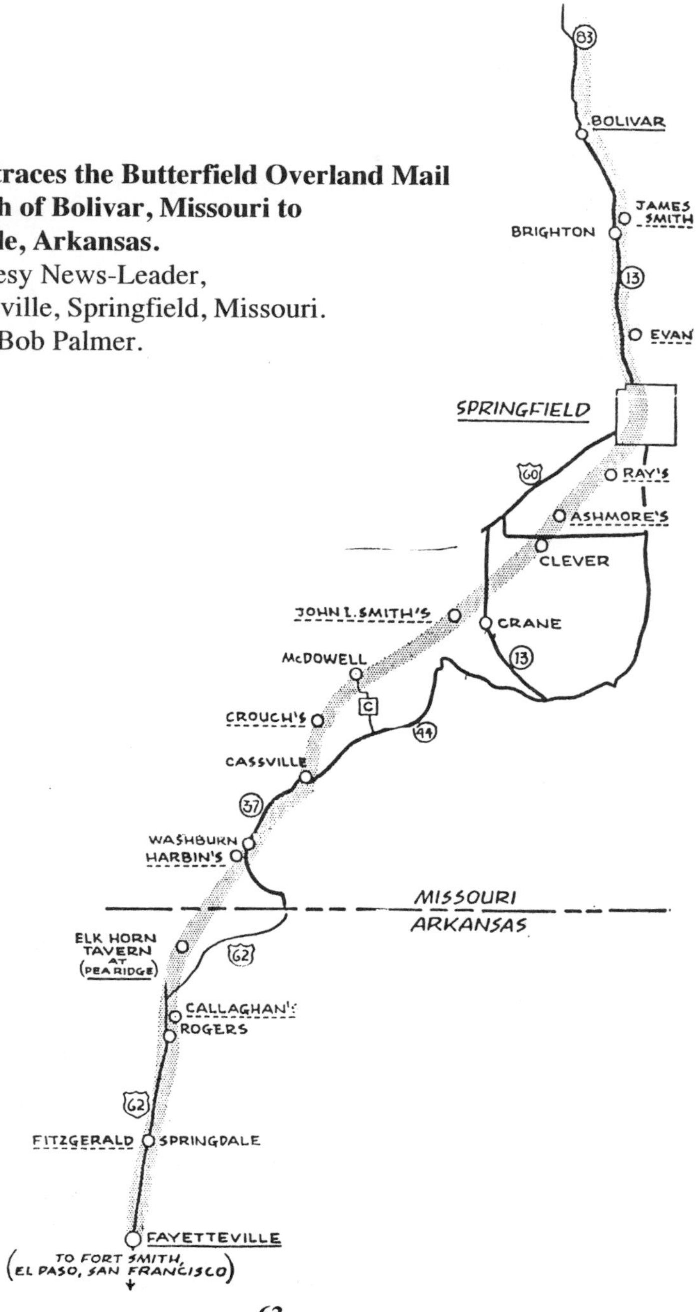

The map traces the Butterfield Overland Mail from north of Bolivar, Missouri to Fayetteville, Arkansas.
Map courtesy News-Leader,
651 Booneville, Springfield, Missouri.
Drawn by Bob Palmer.

BOLIVAR

JAMES SMITH

BRIGHTON

EVAN

SPRINGFIELD

RAY'S

ASHMORE'S

CLEVER

JOHN L.SMITH'S

CRANE

McDOWELL

CROUCH'S

CASSVILLE

WASHBURN
HARBIN'S

MISSOURI
ARKANSAS

ELK HORN
TAVERN
AT
(PEA RIDGE)

CALLAGHAN'S
ROGERS

FITZGERALD   SPRINGDALE

FAYETTEVILLE
TO FORT SMITH,
(EL PASO, SAN FRANCISCO)

**Butterfield Overland Mail
The map pictured traces the mail route
from Tipton, Missouri,
to McDowell, in Barry County.**

The map was reprinted courtesy the
News-Leader, Springfield, Missouri.
Bob Palmer was the cartoonist.

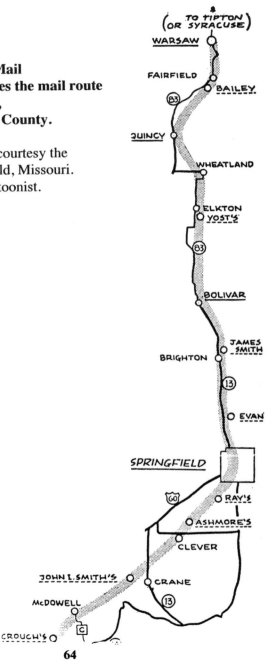

Missouri Had First Stations on the Overland Stage Route

CALIF.
San Francisco
Los Angeles
ARIZ.
Fort Yuma
Tucson
Apache Pass
N.MEX.
El Paso
TEXAS
MO.
St. Louis
Tipton
Springfield
OKLA.
Fayetteville
Fort Smith
Boggy Depot
ARK.
Colberts Ferry
Sherman

shrill sound of the bugle announced the approaching stage coach. Stops were made for meals and the changing of horses only.

Two types of coaches were used, the Concord coach, made at Concord, New Hampshire, and the 'celerity' (mud) wagon manufactured at Troy, New York. The former, a regular full-bodied coach weighed 3,000 pounds, and had a capacity of about two tons, cost approximately $1,400, and could accommodate six to nine passengers inside and quite a number on top. This stage was made of the finest ash, oak, elm, and prime basswood. These coaches were designed for comfort, and made by the famous Abbot-Downing Company; the light, elegant, and durable vessels revolutionized western travel.

The Abbot-Downing coaches made for the Butterfield Company were painted in bright colors, usually red, green, or canary yellow. The wheels were heavy, with broad iron tires that

65

would not sink in the soft sand, and set wide enough apart—five feet, two inches—to keep the coach from tipping. The body, reinforced with iron, was swung on leather straps, or through braces stitched three and one-fourth inches wide. The cab rocked back and forth as the coach bowled forward, the through braces acting as shock absorbers. The more elegant Concord coaches were used only at the end of the route, but on the rougher sections of the road, from Ft. Smith, Arkansas, to Los Angeles, California, passengers and mail were shifted to carriages of the specially built 'celerity' or mud wagons. These were much like the regular coaches in appearance except for smaller wheels and a frame top structure covered with heavy duck. Also, they had three seats inside which could be adjusted to form a bed where passengers could sleep in relay. Heavy leather, or duck, curtains protected the passengers from rain or cold. The interior of both types were lined with russet leather with cushions of the same material. Illumination was furnished by candle lamps.

The vehicles were pulled by four to six horses, or mules, and rolled day and night except for brief stops for meals or a change of horses. Their speed varied from four miles in rough country to twelve miles per hour over level stretches of prairie or down long slopes. In 24 hours the stage covered approximately 120 miles. Passengers paid $200 to ride the entire distance westward, $100 to ride back. This was later adjusted to $150 each way. The Post Office paid $600,000 a year for handling the mail. John Butterfield spent more than one million dollars from the time he signed the contract to a year later when service began.

Passengers on the first Butterfield Overland Mail trip which began September 16, 1858, were John Butterfield, President of the company; Mr. and Mrs. John F. Wheeler and their two children from Ft. Smith, Arkansas; T. R. Corbin, Washington, D.C.; Waterman Ormsby, a reporter from the New York Herald newspaper and the conductor. All of the passengers except Ormsby got off the stage at Ft. Smith, Arkansas.

Mail and passengers from Memphis, Tennessee, traveled to Des Arc, Arkansas, by steamboat. From that point they were transferred to a stage coach line which carried them to Ft. Smith, Arkansas, where the Butterfield line was met for the westward trip.

Scene of changing stagecoach for celerity wagon.

The Overland Mail crossing stream at night (1858)

In addition to the regular scheduled stops, many unscheduled stops were made. Leaving Springfield and heading south, the coaches made the first unscheduled stop at the John A Ray home near Wilson's Creek. A Post Office was located there from 1856-1866. The next stop was on the regular schedule. It was at the John C. Ashmore Station, some 16 miles south of Springfield, and only a few miles northeast of Clever, Missouri.

At one time an unscheduled stop was at the Robert Teague store which was also the site of the Curran Post Office. This stop was in Christian County, just inside the Christian-Stone County line. The old Cristoe church was also at this location where it stood for many years before decaying and falling to the ground. Gene Hair, grandson of Robert Teague, remembers hearing that his grandfather sold tickets for the Butterfield Overland Mail. The Curran Post Office was later moved to Stone County where it remained in different locations for many years. From the Christian-Stone County line the Butterfield Overland Mail traveled southward to a small store owned and operated by a Mr. Talley. There is no indication that this was a mail stop.

The next unscheduled stop was at the Alexander McCullah Settlement, one mile west of Brown's Spring, Missouri. Alexander McCullah, born 1793 in Virginia, died in 1856, Stone County, Missouri without knowing what an important part the McCullah Settlement would play in Civil War years.

The Curran Post Office was located at the Alexander McCullah Settlement from 1853-1856. The site of the small village cannot be reached by a road today. It is difficult to imagine that the bugle blast announcing the arrival of the Butterfield Overland Mail, and the firing of artillery during a skirmish between the Federal and the Confederate forces were heard by residents of the town. The map on page 66 was drawn by Miss Ursula (called Sulie) Thompson, whose relatives lived at the settlement from 1877-1882. Ursula, the daughter of Elijah and Louisa Thompson, taught school in the area for 23 years and served at the Hurley Post Office for 13 years. Strangely, the directions on the map are transposed. Reading from the bottom of the page upward, the map is looking south. We are indebted to the late Curtis Davis, Crane, Missouri, for the unpublished map of the **McCullah** Settlement. Special thanks are

Marker at the Ashmore Station, a short distance from Clever, Mo.

Marker near the site of the John C. Ashmore Station.

69

Map of McCullah Settlement by Ursula Thompson

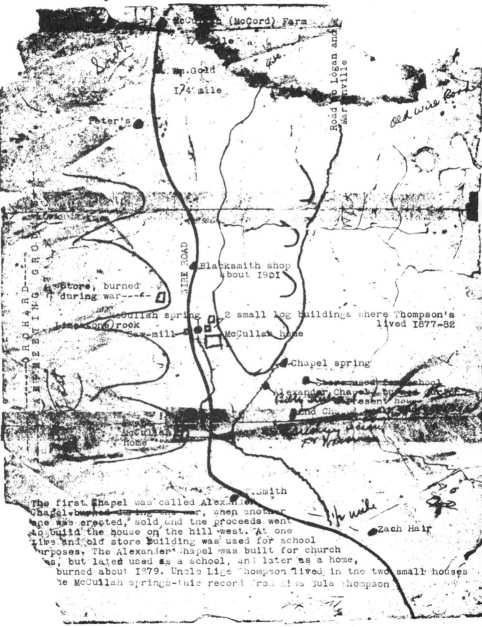

McCullah (McCord) Farm

1/2 mile

Wm.Gold

1/4 mile

Peter's

Road to Logan and Marionville

Old Wire Road

South

WIRE ROAD

Blacksmith shop
about 1901

Store, burned
during war---←---

McCullah spring

2 small log buildings where Thompson's
lived 1877-82

Lime stone rock

Saw-mill

McCullah home

Chapel spring

Store used for school

Alexander Chapel burned

and Ch

McCullah
home

ORCHARD
CAMPMEETING GROUND

Smith

Zach Hair

The first Chapel was called Alexander
Chapel burned during the war, when another
one was erected, sold and the proceeds went
to build the house on the hill west. At one
time and old store building was used for school
purposes. The Alexander Chapel was built for church
as, but later used as a school, and later as a home,
burned about 1879. Uncle Lige Thompson lived in the two small houses
he McCullah springs-this record from Miss Sula Thompson

70

1906—Ursula Lee Thompson, "Aunt Sula."

also due Irene Langley, Hurley, from whom information of the map was obtained.

The next stop, also unscheduled, of the Butterfield Overland Mail was at the Wesley McCullah Stop, some three miles on down the valley. Wesley, son of Alexander McCullah, was appointed military Postmaster of the Curran office in 1862. He was killed by a lawless band in 1865.

John I. Smith, who operated Smith's Tavern, or Inn, in Barry County was born in Bedford, Tennessee. This was a regular scheduled stop on the line, a large spring furnished plenty of water there.

From the Smith Tavern the mail route traveled to Madry, down Camp Bliss hollow to McDowell, and up Big Flat Creek to a stop at the John D. Crouch station south of Cassville. From the Crouch station the route continued across Washburn Prairie to another regular stop. This station was operated by John H. Harbin, and was the last stop in Missouri. Leaving Barry County via the Rock Creek Road, the route entered Arkansas six miles south of the Harbin stop and continued on in the direction of Pea Ridge, Arkansas. After reaching Fayetteville and Ft. Smith, the route began its western journey to San Francisco, California.

For the next two and one-half years, 1859-1861, the mail and passenger route grew and prospered; the movement to the western states was in full swing. However dissension over the location of the southern route had been brewing for some time; new bills had been passed in Congress ordering the Butterfield Overland Mail to abandon the southern route and follow a central direction.

During the last days of the Butterfield Overland Mail in Missouri, the unrest of the Civil War was causing trouble along the line. Mail coaches had been stopped by outlaw bands at Ft. Smith,

Crouch Station in Barry County, Mo.

72

Indians attacking an Overland Express coach.

Arkansas, and at Tuscon, Arizona. The strain of the project broke John Butterfield physically, and he retired from the presidency of the company in 1860. The last load of scheduled passengers arrived back in Missouri on March 21, 1861, and the last mail from Missouri arrived in California on April 1, 1861.

The assets of the Butterfield were transferred to the St. Joseph-Sacramento line and overland mail from St. Joseph, Missouri, to Sacramento, California, via Virginia, Nevada, and Salt Lake, Utah, began in July, 1861.

In January, 1865, some four years after the Butterfield Overland Mail was discontinued, still another stage line was resumed from Springfield to Cassville, Missouri, over the Wire Road. Instead of following the previous stagecoach route from Cassville, it went to Fayetteville, Arkansas, along changed markings.

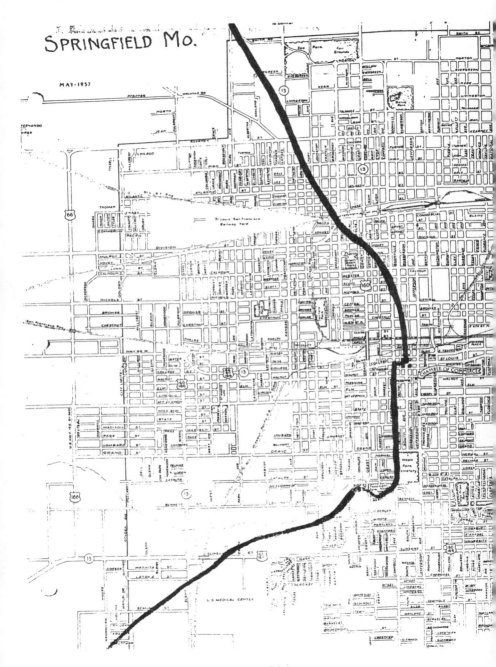

SPRINGFIELD MO.

MAY-1957

The Butterfield Overland Mail Through
Springfield, Missouri

The Butterfield Overland Mail entered northwest Springfield via the old Booneville, or Bolivar Road. As with the Wire Road, almost all traces of the old route have been obliterated.

Crossing Kearney Street, a short distance west of North Fort Street, it continued to Commercial Street and Broadway Avenue. From there it traveled south and east, and entered Booneville Avenue (then Booneville Road) at Nichols Street, present location of the Greene County Court House. It then proceeded south on Booneville to the Public Square and a scheduled stop at the Nicholas Smith Hotel, on the northeast corner of Booneville and the Public Square.

Looking down the Wire Road in 1992.

The coaches then traveled two blocks west to Campbell, where they turned south passing by Maple Park Cemetery on the east side of Campbell Avenue. A semi-circle in the route led by

Butterfield Overland Mail marker in North Springfield.

Fassnight Park on the north side of the road. From this point the Butterfield Overland Mail continued southwest crossing Sunshine Street a short distance east of Scenic Street. The road then cut across property now owned by the present United States Medical Center and left Springfield on its way across Greene and other counties.

Curran, Missouri Post Office

The small post office of Curran played an important role in the history of Stone County, Missouri, which had been organized in 1851. Documents obtained from the National Archives are listed below.

Crane Creek, Missouri	
Parrington Packwood (P M)	7 January, 1853
Discontinued 4 September, 1855	
Moved to Curran	
Alexander McCullah	6 September, 1853
James A. McCullah	20 May, 1856
William F. McCullah	12 April, 1859
John W. McCullah	11 July, 1862
James W. McCullah	13 January, 1865
Jesse P. Williams	5 July, 1856
Moved to Barry County	5 July, 1866
Reestablished in Stone County	
Theodore C. Mitchell	23 February, 1872
John C. King	1 October, 1874
Discontinued	3 February, 1875
Reestablished	7 May, 1875
George Burk	7 May, 1875
Discontinued	17 October, 1881
Reestablished	22 December, 1886
Sarah E. King	22 December, 1886
Discontinued	16 September, 1895
Patrons sent to Bradfield, Missouri	

Butterfield Stage Route Through Barry County

The map below was prepared some time ago through research by the staff of the Cassville Republican. The names of most of the smaller towns in the county are shown on the map together with the date of the first place of business or the date of the plat together with the original name of the town.

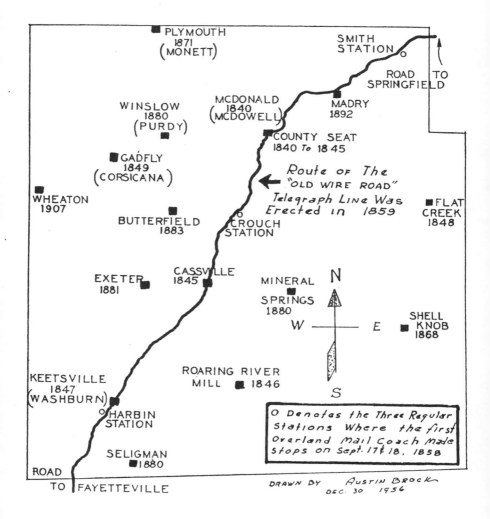

Chapter Six

They Helped Blaze The Trail

Dr. John William King - 1869: "I won't live in a country where human bones litter the roadways."

They Helped Blaze The Trail

Though the documentation in the following chapter may seem quite local, the experiences of these families who lived along, or near, the Wire Road could have happened to ancestors in any part of the Missouri Ozarks. The information is included to paint a picture of the honest, thrifty, God-fearing, early settlers who came to this untamed area firmly believing, "Where there is a will, there is a way." With determination, and by the sweat of their brow, these hardy pioneers overcame the many obstacles they encountered while carving a home for themselves and their families from the vast wilderness that we know as the Missouri Ozarks today.

To those who are documented here, and to others living along the Wire Road from St. Louis, to Ft. Smith, Arkansas, we say, "Thank you for helping blaze the trial, and for a job well done." Thanks are also due to the descendants of these people who so willingly provided information and pictures for the book.

They Helped Blaze The Trail

1. Rufus Burton Brown
2. John C. Estes
3. John Benjamin Hair
4. William Eli Hair
5. William (Bud) Hair
6. Zachariah Hair
7. John W. King
8. Harold Henderson Leake
9. Jesse Thomas Martin
10. Thomas J. McCord
11. Alexander McCullah
12. James Alexander McCullah
13. John Wesley McCullah
14. John I.Smith*
15. John Short
16. Thomas D. Smith
17. Manlius Steele

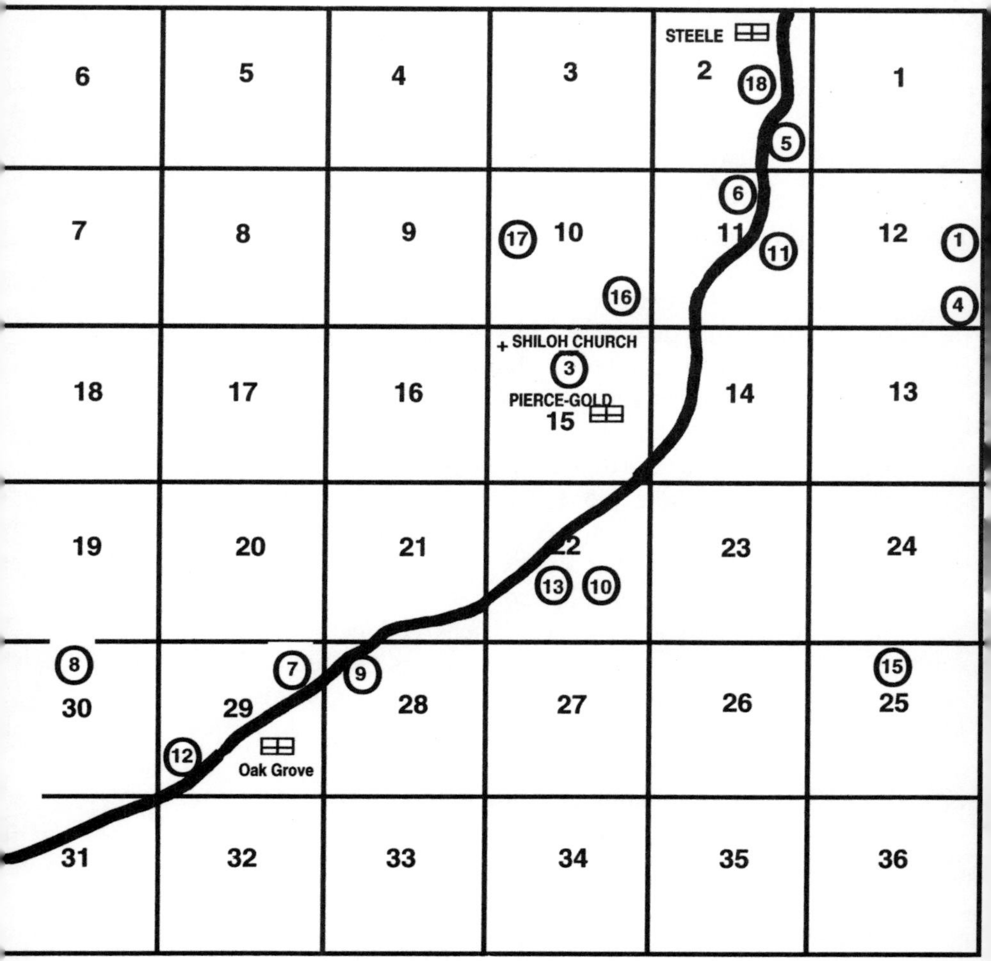
STEELE
6
5
4
3
2
18
1
5
6
7
8
9
17
10
11
11
12
1
16
4
SHILOH CHURCH
3
PIERCE-GOLD
18
17
16
15
14
13
19
20
21
22
23
24
13
10
8
7
9
15
30
29
28
27
26
25
12
Oak Grove
31
32
33
34
35
36

18.   William Steele

*Lived in Barry County (all others listed lived in Stone County)

Rufus Burton Brown
1821-1906

Rufus Burton Brown, his wife Ruth Barnes Brown, and their three children came to the Missouri Ozarks from North Carolina in 1852. Although a large spring was located on the property where Rufus Brown settled, and it must have been a decisive asset, the prime reason that the family came to Stone County was that Burton Brown had been granted a claim as compensation for military service. The Bounty Land Claim, filed in Springfield, Missouri, in 1852, stated: "Rufus Brown entered the service as a private in a Regiment of the North Carolina Volunteers, in 1838, for the purpose of moving the Cherokee." The claim location was described in detail, listing section, township, and range. This was not the only service that Burton Brown rendered his country. In 1862, he enlisted in the Missouri State Militia Cavalry, United States Army and was honorably discharged in 1865.

The Rufus Burton Brown farm was located a short distance from the old Wire Road. A small log building, using wooden pegs instead of nails, still stands on the former Brown property, now owned by the Lee DeWitt family.

Because of an abundance of water, a small settlement known as Brown's Spring grew up in the vicinity. The small village once boasted a school, church, several stores, and a canning factory. Today only a few houses remain to remind one of the activities of the past.

Five generation descendants of the Burton Browns are still living in Stone County, Missouri. Rufus Brown died in 1906.

Helen Baker Carney

John C. and Margaret Estes
1796-1880   1798-1880

The Estes family were among the early settlers who emigrated from Roane and Morgan County, Tennessee. Hardin and Sarah Estes Coffer and two children came to Missouri in 1849. Three brothers; Paul, Samuel, and John H. Estes; Johnson and Elizabeth Ann Estes White, and family followed. Later the parents, John C. and Margaret Estes and their children; Nancy Margaret, Martha A., and Eliza came and settled in this area. The oldest son, Peter Estes remained in Tennessee. Other descendants of the Estes family are living today in Coalfield, Tennessee.

Paul Estes settled two and one-half miles southeast of Clever, Missouri, at that time there was no other settlement between there and Marionville. This farm became known as the Estes homestead; Robert Estes, known as "Big Bob" lived on the farm until his death. Since then the property has passed down through several Estes generations.

John Wiley Estes, son of Paul and Paulina Carpenter Estes operated a flour mill in Union City in 1902. Union City was then known as School, Missouri. This mill was operated by a sixty-horsepower, wood-fixed steam engine, its capacity was fifty barrels per day. Later, it was moved to Clever and the capacity was increased to one hundred twenty-five barrels per day. Many Estes descendants still live in southwest Missouri today.

Marjorie Hair Thornton

John Benjamin Hair

John Benjamin and Nancy J. Forrester Hair moved from Lincoln County to Memphis, Tennessee, where their first child, Mary Jane, was born. From there, they came to Missouri and settled in northern Stone County, near Curran. Later, a brother, Zachariah, sister Mary, and the Forrester family came to Stone County.

John Benjamin Hair served in the Civil War with Captain Moore's Independent Company and the Stone County Regiment of the Missouri Home Guards, where he was wounded. The Hair family was then living near Russell Hill, southeast of Crane, Missouri. At one time a group of Confederate soldiers captured a Union soldier and brought him to the Hair Home. The Captain of the group demanded that Nancy Hair cook them a chicken dinner. She complied. Later that evening the Confederate soldiers decided to kill the Yankee and ordered young Eli Hair to bring them a pick and shovel. The following morning the soldier was hung and was buried on the Hair property. The group then rode away.

Children of John Benjamin and Nancy Hair were as follows: Mary Jane, William Eli, Mason, and Francis.

Marjorie Thornton Hair

Shiloh Church, near the Wire Road, celebrated its 100th anniversary in 1989. The land for the church was donated by John Benjamin Hair.

William Eli Hair
1854-1919

William Eli Hair married Mary Susan Teague. They settled in Brown's Spring, Missouri, and started housekeeping in a log cabin with a lean-to and a dirt floor. Eli drove a freight wagon from Springfield, Missouri, to Eureka Springs, Arkansas, and also farmed. He later bought a hundred and twenty acres of land for one dollar per acre in 1896, and built the large Hair home. The home is still standing, in good repair, at the south end of Main Street, Brown's Spring, not far from the old Wire Road.

Children of Eli and Mary Susan Hair were as follows: Nancy Louiza, Francis Marion, Ellen, Gertrude Susan, and Leonard Charles.

Marjorie Hair Thornton

Zachariah Hair
1833-1911

Zachariah Hair was born October 2, 1833, in Lincoln County, Tennessee. His parents were John William and Louiza Hair. Zachariah served in the Civil War in Captain Moore's Independent Company, Stone County Regiment, Missouri Home Guards.

The first marriage of Zachariah Hair was to Mary Emaline Sullivan on January 10, 1854. They had three children, John W Hair, William (Bud) Hair, and Martha Jane Hair. The second wife of Zachariah Hair was Nancy Cunningham; they were married January 11, 1899.

William (Bud) Hair, born September 11, 1863, son of Zachariah and Mary Hair, was married (1) Lou Hodges, (2) Dora Pearce, (3) Dora Hays. Many of the stories of happenings along the Wire Road were related by "Uncle Bud" Hair to his son, Evert Hair. The Hair families were residents of northern Stone County for many years.

Emma Lou Hair Barnett

John William King
1820-1884

John William King, his wife Sara Elizabeth, and four children left their home in Mobile, Alabama, and on March 17, 1868, settled on a 169 acre farm two miles north of Crane, Missouri. The farm was purchased from Benjamin and Polly Wheeler.

The Wire Road ran directly through the King farm. Helen (King) Ellis, granddaughter of John W. and Sara Elizabeth King, remembers that her grandparents often told of the rubbish of all kinds that was found along the old Wire Road—broken guns, wagon wheels and other parts, broken pieces of harness, saddles, old leather shoes, and signs of meals being cooked over camp fires.

The grandparents of Helen (King) Ellis also told of the Indians on the Trail of Tears. "The trail was rocky, hilly, and full of holes and the road was hard packed. There were many wild animals along the road which the Indians killed for their food. They were only allowed to get a short distance from the trail. A few did manage to escape. One Indian man who lived in the community was thought to have been an escapee. He left the area for a short time and returned with bullets made of lead. Many people, even today, are looking for the source of the bullets, but none have been found. The Indian man is buried in the Oak Grove Cemetery."

John William King, unaccustomed to the rocks, timber, and cold climate returned to his plantation in Mobile, Alabama, after one year in Missouri. On one occasion he remarked that he did not like a country where human bones were scattered along the roadway.

Sara Elizabeth King remained on the farm with her children. On December 22, 1886, she was commissioned postmaster of the Curran Post Office, by William F. Viles. She held this position until her sudden illness and death on June 26, 1901. The Curran Post Office was closed after her death and was never reopened.

Clarence A. King, son of John W. King, continued to live on the farm and taught two terms of school at the Oak Grove School for a salary of $23 per month. Later he enrolled in Tulane Medical College, New Orleans, Louisiana. After receiving a medical diploma in 1892, he practiced medicine in Rogers, Arkansas. There

86

he met and married Lillie D. Bennett formerly of Vicksburg, Mississippi. They returned to his farm near Crane and purchased a total of 997-1/2 acres of land on both sides of the road which is now Highway 13. Dr. Clarence King continued to practice medicine, farm, and raise cattle. In later years Dr. King was ship surgeon on several ships, traveling all over the world. Besides treating patients in this area he practiced in Lawrence County and in several southern states.

Lillie D. (Bennett) King died in 1934; Dr. Clarence King died in 1940. The large acreage of land was divided by the four children: Jewell, Ruby, Champ, and Helen. Jewell, Ruby and Champ are deceased.

Clarence and Helen (King) Ellis have owned the farm since 1934. They had one son, Ronald D., who now resides at home with his mother.

Ronald D. Ellis is the fourth generation of the King family to occupy the 123 year old farm. The King-Ellis farm received a plaque in 1988, which designates it as a Century Farm Club Award farm. The marker may be seen in the yard of the Helen and Ronald Ellis home, two miles north of Crane, on Highway 13. The Wire Road running down the Ellis driveway, just south of the house, is plainly visible there today.

Helen King Ellis

Harold Henderson and Dorothy Leake
1891-1978   1893-1990

A Wire Road Romance

In 1920 when Benjamin Franklin VanDyke, father of Dorothy VanDyke Leake, bought the old Wisman Mill acreage at the headwaters of Crane creek, he was happy that his daughter and her husband Harold Henderson Leake with their small daughter could come to live there. Dorothy had come to southwest Missouri from western Oklahoma to attend Drury College in Springfield, Missouri. Harold was a native of Aurora. They met as freshmen students at Drury. For Dorothy and Harold, who had discovered the property, it was a dream-come-true. For both it had a rich historical heritage and was a paradise of native plants and animals.

The Wire Road, only two miles to the south, had served the Butterfield Stage along that road. Harold, familiar with the hand-in-glove operation between the railroads and telegraph, delved into stage-coach stops along Wire Road. Harold's father, John Leake, had been a Frisco agent when Harold was a small tyke. Learning the history of Wire Road was like exploring the beginnings of telegraphy in pre-railroad transportation.

During the early 1920's, Harold wrote a column for the Crane Chronicle often featuring farm families that had originally settled along the old trail which had become Wire Road. These columns contained reminiscences of the telegraph and the Butterfield Stage. Some could remember troop movements along the road and the misery endured on the Cherokee Trail of Tears. Some noted that springs along the route became more or less permanent camp sites.

In about 1901, railroad expansion brought the present line that crosses Wire Road at Little Crane through the Ozarks for the purpose of harvesting hard-wood trees for railroad ties. The oak-hickory forests were clear-cut and much farm land opened. Blasting of the bluff at Big Spring, headwaters of Crane Creek resulted in blockage of the spring to make a roadbed for the rails. The fill deprived "hound runners" of a favorite camp site on the bluff. The spring triumphed, gushing from below the railroad track, it brought two or three floods a year.

The Wisman family removed to property below Crane because maintenance of the mill pond at the Big Spring for power was too costly. Over the years, the VanDyke-Leake family has discovered three different sets of dam pilings, uncovered by flooding of the tributaries to Crane Creek, closer and closer to the Big Spring. Progressively the mill was moved downstream.

The older historical heritage of Wire Road abides with the families descended from early settlers.

Love of the natural setting resulted in the book *Flowering Plants of the Ozarks*, illustrated by Dorothy with text by Harold. Following Harold's death, Dorothy fell in love with the plants of the southwest United States desert. Currently in press is *Desert and Mountain Plants of the Southwestern United States*. Dorothy is, of course, the primary author for both drawings and text, but she graciously extended co-authorship to her daughter and son.

Dorothy VanDyke and Harold Henderson Leake bequeathed to Marcelotte Leake Roeder and John Benjamin Leake, their children, the rich heritage of the Wire Road area. They will endeavor to restore its natural beauty and preserve the Wire Road heritage.

Marcelotte Leake Roeder

Jesse Thomas Martin
1854-1919

Jesse Thomas Martin was born January 11, 1854. He was the son of Jesse Ransom and Catherine Martin. In 1896 he married Sarah Ann Gipson.

After the marriage of Jesse Thomas and Sarah Ann Gipson, the couple purchased 120 acres of land adjoining the old Wire Road. Here they raised their family of 12 children. The farm was located in the Oak Grove community, about two miles north of Crane, Missouri. The Martin children recalled playing with lead mini-balls that they found along the old road.

Ransom Martin, father of Jesse, enlisted in the First Arkansas Cavalry on August 4, 1862. He was a Private in Company H. commanded by Captain John I. Worthington. The First Arkansas Cavalry—twelve units in all—was mustered into Federal service at Springfield, on August 7, 1862.

Jesse Thomas and Sarah worked hard to raise crops and provide food for their large family. The Martin children recall how they peeled 20-30 bushels of apples at one time with the help of friends and neighbors. The fruit was then dried and stored for winter use.

Betty Martin Henry

Dr. T. J. McCord

Conscripted by the Confederate Army when only sixteen years old, T. J. McCord ran away and joined the Union Army where he served until the end of the Civil War four years later. He moved to Stone County, Missouri, from Clarksville, Arkansas, his family having located here in 1836. After the war, T. J. McCord attended the University Medical School, Ann Arbor, Michigan, and graduated with a doctor's degree.

Dr. Thomas J. McCord

Nannie Carr McCord

Dr. T. J. McCord married Nancy Armina Carr on January 14, 1872. The following children were born to the McCords: Fred, Charles Calvin, Vinnie Ethel, LeRoy Jefferson, Thomas J., Lois, Helen, and Kathryn. In 1873, he opened a drug store in Galena, Missouri.

John Wesley and Melcena Short McCullah had moved to Stone County in 1852, where they operated the McCullah Stop, on the Wire Road. The place was a stopping place for the Butterfield Overland Mail. After the death of Wesley McCullah, at the hands of bushwhackers, the property was purchased by Francis (Frank) and T. J. McCord. It was located northwest of Hurley, Missouri, and contained several hundred acres of land. The property became known as the McCord Ranch, a name it retains today.

When the McCord family purchased the large ranch, it had a double log house and a barn, in addition to the store. Dr. McCord continued to practice in the surrounding neighborhood. The country at that time was sparsely settled, physicians were few and far between. A few families who had brought with them their colored help and customs of the deep south had already settled in the valley where wood and water were plentiful. The McCords, having been reared in the south, soon employed a large family of Negroes, the Neel Carters. The family came to Missouri from Arkansas, and lived in a tenant house near the northwest line and in sight of the present house. The Neel Carter family is listed in the 1880 Census of Stone County. They are buried in unmarked graves in nearby Oak Grove cemetery.

The Historic McCord Residence

The house built by the McCords has attracted admiration and historical interest for many years. Still standing today, it is said to be the finest old house in Stone County. Built by Dr. T. J. McCord, it was completed in 1888, after being under construction for two years. It is situated in a valley near a stream known for many years as McCord Branch on an original 1,000 acre tract of land of northern Stone County farm and timberland.

This two story, twelve room house with five porches and a small basement was considered a show place by rural standards of the 1880's. Lumber was plentiful, labor was cheap, and water-powered sawmills could be built on any creek bank. Carpenters took pride in their workmanship in those days. It is said that Dr. McCord sorted every piece of lumber used. Walnut lumber was used extensively throughout, with the exception of one bedroom which was done in pine or red cedar with a complete cedar clothes closet, a novelty is that time.

91

Left to right: Helen (McCord) McCoy and Ruth Asher by the bay window.

The first floor was finished with walnut wainscot. The front entrance hall had a beautiful open stairway on the south side and a parlor room on the north. The hall led into the "sitting" room which had a walnut-paneled fireplace. A large bay window complete with inside shutters faced the south. An archway with inside sliding doors on the north of the "sitting" room opened into a small den, or library.

The large dining room contained the second enclosed stairway leading to the upper story. Outside doors opened to porches on both north and south sides of the house from this room. The kitchen had a fireplace, a huge built-in dough board, flour storage combination, and two antique washstands with red marble bases and round, white porcelain bowls. A large pantry room on the north of the kitchen contained a separate storage closet and an inside stairway to the basement.

The attached well room, with a concrete floor and latticed walls on the east of the house, contained a wider concrete stairway to the basement. The well was hand-dug and lined with layers of rock reaching down many feet.

The second floor consisted of four large bedrooms, a small storage room, Dr. McCord's medicine room, two halls and two

The older children of the Fred McCords: Allen, 7 years, standing; Helen, 5 years; and Lois, 4, side by side; Carl, 2 years, in front.

porches A speaking tube was installed between the first and second floor.

In 1893-1894 the McCord farm and the beautiful old house were sold. The McCords moved to Marionville where Dr. McCord was Coroner of Lawrence County. They later moved to Galena where they spent the rest of their lives. The outside of the house has changed very little; modern conveniences have been added on the inside. In 1919 Fred McCord, son of Dr. McCord, moved to the large acreage. The move from Galena to the McCord Ranch was made in wagons and required a full day. Fred McCord was a stockman, shipping large numbers of livestock to the markets in Kansas City, Missouri. Stock was driven from the large ranch to the railroad stockyards in Crane, via the large north hill and on down Main Street. Few, if any, automobiles were parked on the streets at that time. People lent a helping hand in those days.

Fred McCord (1876-1962) pictured in 1900.

In January, 1951, the McCord Ranch passed to new owners after having been in the McCord family for over three-quarters of a century. Present owners (1992) are Robert and Helen Spellman.

Helen McCord McCoy

Alexander McCullah
1793-1856

Alexander McCullah was born July 16, 1793, in Wythe County, Virginia. He was the son of Alexander and Rebecca Wheat McCullah. He died April 18, 1856. Due to a severe drought in Virginia, the family left their home and moved to Tennessee. Alexander joined the U. S. Army and fought in the war of 1812, serving under Colonel Blue, a regiment under the command of General Andrew Jackson. He served as a private in Captain Rogers' Company of the Tennessee Militia. He was discharged in 1815; for his services he received a military grant signed by President Buchanan which he applied to land in Stone County, Missouri.

Alexander McCullah married Lucy Robertson in 1819, and moved to Stone County in 1850. The McCullah home was located near a large spring. It was used as a tavern in the stagecoach days and was burned after the Civil War. He built the first chapel and schoolhouse in Stone County. The McCullah Settlement was a stopping place on the Butterfield Overland Mail route which later became known as the Wire Road.

Lucy, wife of Alexander McCullah died in 1849. He later married Elizabeth Coleman. Their children were as follows: Elizabeth, John Wesley, Rebecca, Thomas Lindsay, James Alexander, Lucinda Caroline, William Francis, Rufus Asbury, and Samuel Calvin.

Mary Lois McCullah Kelley

The students of Chapel School in 1922 have been identified by Ralph Smith, Sacramento, Calif. Front row, left to right: Bessie Maples, Beaula Welch, Helen Gray, Lula Maples, Wilbur Hair, Howard Adams, Jones Chastain, Ralph Smith, Howard Hair, Edward Adams.

Second row, left to right: Burl Bettes, Gray McCull Leon Livingston, Haywood Smith, Melvin Gold, Norm Bond, Gorden Chastain, Lyman Maples.

Third row, left to right: Teacher Cecil Dean, Irene Ho ard, Ivon Steele, Ester Adams, Opel Sullivan, Julie Pete Gene Welch, Claude Pierce, Donald Hair, Efton Livingst Teacher Rosco Wiley.

Fourth row, left to right: Cecil Gold, May Peters, Mildr Peters, Linda Pierce, Myrtle Howard, Hazel Chastain, He Livingston, Miera Steele.

Fifth row, left to right: Grace Robinson, Oma McConn Richard Welch, Lowel Peters, Wayne Bettes, Garfield Mi Roy Bettes, John Steele.

The first Chapel school was a log building built by Alexander McCullah. The second building was a frame school, the first in Stone County. The children above went to a third Chapel school.

James Alexander McCullah

James Alexander McCullah was born January 18, 1829, Monroe County, Tennessee. He died in Stone County, Missouri, on March 28, 1901. He came to Missouri with his parents in 1849 and

96

was married to Idella A. Parks in 1860. Both are buried in the Oak Grove Cemetery, near Crane, Missouri.

James A. McCullah entered the Federal Service of the Stone County Home Guards in May 1861, and remained in that organization until August, 1862, when he joined the Enrolled Militia and was afterward appointed Deputy Provost Marshall, and served in that capacity until the close of the Civil War. He was a Representative of Stone County to the thirty-sixth General Assembly of the State Legislature in 1891-1892. He worked for the Internal Revenue Department for several years. He was a strong Union man, as were all of his brothers. He served as Postmaster of Curran as did his father, Alexander, and several other McCullah relatives.

James McCullah was converted at the age of twelve years. Always active in the church, he became an ordained Methodist minister later in life. His daughters recalled that he wore white linen suits in the summer months, these had to be laundered by hand. The girls were careful to see that a white suit was ready and waiting as their father dressed for the pulpit each Sunday morning.

Wire Road Wildlife Area sign. The James A. McCullah farm is now owned by the Missouri Conservation Department. The sign is two miles north of Crane, Missouri on Highway 13.

The James McCullah family purchased a farm on the Old Wire Road near Crane. Crane Creek ran through the McCullah land. It was at this location that the Cherokee camped as they made their way westward. It was also here that soldiers of the Confederate armies combined forces preceding the Battle of Wilson's Creek. This property is now owned by the Missouri Conservation Department and is known as the Wire Road Wildlife Area.

A skirmish was held on February 14, 1862, near the Crane Creek crossing. Fifteen Confederate soldiers were killed and nine were wounded. A local story, handed down by word of mouth, is that when the fighting began the Confederate Army had a wagon load of lead which was too heavy to be moved hurriedly; it was dumped in Crane Creek. Another story is that the Confederates had several loads of corn which they were reluctant to leave behind. The end gates were pulled from the wagons and the precious grain trickled onto the dusty road.

James McCullah built a log schoolhouse a short distance from his home. Nearby, a small cemetery was established in a grove of walnut trees. On the banks of Crane Creek just west of the McCullah home stood a blacksmith shop; near the creek was another building called the ice house. Ice, cut in blocks was cut and stored in the building during the winter months and was used sparingly during the hot summer days.

Pictured is the historical home of James Alexander and Idella Parks McCullah. The large house, a landmark in the area was built in 1885. It was razed in 1961 to make room for the modern, new home of the Leonard Williams family. The house was built on a sloping hill where workmen, using picks and shovels, made a fill by wheeling the dirt in wheel barrows. A rock wall was also constructed by hand labor using no mortar. Laborers worked for fifty cents per day and the noon meal.

The massive house contained seven large and three small rooms. Fires were kindled in two fireplaces in the late afternoon so the rooms would be warm through the night. The floors were insulated with several inches of dirt between the sills. Considered a showplace in its time, the house had many unusual features. The upstairs rooms sloped in at the top and an old-fashioned bay

This picture of the James A. McCullah home was taken in the late twenties. The girl sitting on the fence is Ruth Ellis Baker.

Window was on the west side. Doors, windows, casings, facings, and floors were made of spruce; the hand-made stairway banister was of solid walnut.

Large storage spaces were required for the McCullah family which numbered eleven children. In the kitchen a large bin for flour held one hundred pounds, another similar bin held one hundred pounds of meal. A bell was mounted on top of the house to call the men to dinner. Above the second floor, one small room was called the observatory. Here James McCullah could monitor the work of the hired hands. One room was as a study; it was here that McCullah prepared the sermons that he delivered to the Methodist churches on Sunday.

John Wesley McCullah – 1821-1863

John Wesley McCullah son of Alexander McCullah was born March 12, 1821. He was killed by bushwhackers on October 11, 1864. He had been appointed military Post Master of the Curran Post Office, Stone County, Missouri during the Civil War.

The Butterfield Overland Mail stage coaches stopped at the Wesley McCullah Stop and spring. The broad valley of the Wesley McCullah farm with its abundance of water became a camping place for armies marching to and from battles along the Wire Road.

The large McCullah acreage was later sold to the McCord family and became known as the McCord Ranch. The open valley which had served both the Federal and the Confederate armies then saw herds of cattle peacefully grazing on the lush grass it provided.

Long after the Civil War and the murder of Wesley McCullah, a story was told that at a certain time each night one could hear the steep hill. Passengers could be heard being discharged and loaded. As the creaking doors swung shut, the horses galloped on down the trail. No one ever reported actually seeing the coaches or the riders.

John Short

John Short came to Missouri in 1850, from Roane County, Tennessee. His sister, Melena Short, married John Wesley McCullah who settled near Crane Creek. He was a staunch Union man in the Civil War and once was taken by guerillas ten miles away where he was shot and left for dead. He revived and reached a neighbor's house where his wounds were dressed, and got back home. At another time, another band, after killing Mr. Short's brother-in-law, John Wesley McCullah, came to kill Mr. Short. He was away. They undertook to burn his home and set fire to some bedding. His brave wife grabbed the bedding and dashed outside. It saved the house. The leader of the group said that a woman as brave as that deserved to keep her home and the band retreated.

Once after that, two men came and found Mr. Short at home. While they were trying to disarm him, his young son George, brought his mother an ax.. She killed one with the ax while the other fled.

The Unknown Soldier is buried not far from where he was killed which is near the present site of Hurley, Missouri.

John I. Smith - 1797-1864

John I. Smith was born September 16, 1797, in Bedford County Tennessee. He moved to Indiana, where he lived nine years before relocating in Barry County, Missouri. John I. Smith owned some 1,000 acres of land near Osa, Missouri. Like many others of that day he traveled to California during the Gold Rush. The family owned several slaves, releasing them after the close of the Civil War. From 1858-1860, he operated an inn on the trail that later became a regular stop on the Butterfield Overland Mail route. A large spring furnished water for the teams pulling the mail and passenger coaches. The spring, said to be the source of Little Crane Creek, flowed through Barry and Stone Counties. It was later known as the Wise or Wilkins Spring. It is now owned by Lydia Mourning Clark's son, and called Spring Mourning.

Mr. Smith had a cellar beneath his home; the entrance to the underground cellar was through a trap door near the fireplace. Mr. Smith's wife, Isabelle, would sit on this door in a rocking chair knitting, so no one would suspect that someone was in the cellar below. On October 30, 1864, John I. Smith was near his son-in-law Step Wise's residence when he was shot and killed by a U. S. scout. In the month prior to this tragedy, Mr. Smith's son Granville was discharged from Co. H. Provisional Enrolled Militia, after been in the Union army since May of 1861.

John I. Smith's first marriage was to Barbry Holt, born in Orange County, N. C. and died March of 1841. To this union two sons and three daughters were born. Granville married Sarah Caroline Burrow, Henry died at age 18, Mary Sue married Charles Newton Gammill, Elizabeth married William Neill, and Sarah Ann married Stephen Wise.

John I. Smith's second wife was to Isabelle Leath, daughter of Hiram Leath, born in Tennessee and to this union was born a son James and a daughter Anna. Mr. Smith was not married a third time as previously listed.

The following are buried at Osa cemetery: John I. and wife Isabelle Smith, Granville Smith, Elizabeth Smith Neill, and Sarah Ann Smith Wise. (Update provided by Betty Marshall Ergovich a great great granddaughter of John I. and Barbry Holt Smith.)

JOHN I SMITH BUTTERFIELD OVERLAND MAIL STAGE-STOP STATION 1858-1861

Thomas D. Smith – 1851-1925

Thomas D. Smith was born December 24, 1851. He was married to Sarah E, Watkins on April 26, 1874. Sarah was born July 24, 1852. The couple was married by Judge James A. McCullah. To this union were born six children: Gertie May, Clara, William F., Samuel, Robert Efton, and Thomas Homer.

The Thomas D. Smith property was located in Township 26, Range 24, Section 10, in Stone County, Missouri. The land was purchased from the St. Louis-San Francisco Railroad for $1.25 per acre. A two room log house with a fireplace in each end was constructed. Later, a frame house was built on the site.

Children of Thomas and Sarah Smith attended the old McCullah Chapel School near Chapel Spring. The Wire Road was close by this location. Children of Robert Efton and Birdie Lora Smith, Haywood and Ralph, attended a later Chapel School built to the west of the old school and McCullah Settlement. This school building has also been discarded and torn down.

Ralph E. Smith

Manlius (Manley) Steele – 1851-1922

Manlius (Manley) Steele married Mary Jane Estes, daughter of Paul and Pauline (Carpenter) Estes, January 11, 1870. They lived in a small farmhouse and later built the larger Steele home some time before 1893. This was located north of the Shiloh Baptist Church, near the community of Bradsfield, Missouri. This location was about one mile west of the Old Wire Road.

Manley was a small man in stature; he had many friends who called him "Uncle Man". Manley liked to read the Cappers Weekly and his Bible. He belonged to the Marionville IOOF Lodge, Chapter 210.

Manley Steele had many friends and would often go to Cassville to visit with a Negro friend whose last name was Rich. He and his family belonged to the Cumberland Presbyterian Church, but they often attended revivals in the neighborhood churches. Sometimes the ministers were invited to spend a few days at the Steele home. The Steels daughters—Anna Lou, Lucy and Mollie—remembered that these visits made extra household work. Floors had to be scrubbed, large meals of fried chicken, home made biscuits, gravy and mashed potatoes were served along with desserts of pies and cakes. In spite of the extra work, the Steele home was noted for its hospitality.

Grandpa Manley read a lot. Sometimes the children would run in and out of the doors during the summer time. They knew when to stop as Grandpa looked down over his glasses on his nose and sternly said, "Here-here!" Children of Manlius and Mary Jane Steele were as follows: William Columbus, Mary, Anna Lou, Robert M., George P., Lucy Ellen, Mary Frances, Alfred Sidney, Finis E., Velma Ethel and Hulda Pearl.

Marjorie Hair Thornton

William J. Steele - 1823-1884

Another settler by the old trail which later became the Wire Road was William J. Steele. Born May 3, 1823, he was the son of Richard and Margaret Steele, of Williamson County, Tennessee.

Richard Steele and his family had come to Greene County some time before 1834. Children of Richard and Margaret were as follows: Richard Steele Jr., who remained in Williamson County, William J., David, John P., Ninian, Margaret, Ann Mary (Polly), Nancy, Eleanor and Rebecca.

William J. Steele married Lucinda J. Beatie in Greene County, Missouri. The family lived near Wilson's Creek before moving to Stone County where they homesteaded land near Brown's Spring, Missouri. Here they built a three room log cabin with a large porch and a chimney in every room. A storage for applies and vegetables was underneath the front porch. The Steele family had two Negro slaves named Alex and Henderson; they had been given to them by Richard Steele, father of William. A separate cabin was built for the Negro families, and also a barn.

William J. Steele was licensed to become a minister by the Ozark Presbytery on October 2, 1846, by the banner of Pearce and Cumberland Presbyterian Advocate, Wilson County, Tennessee. He became known as the Reverend Billy Steele and was also a school teacher.

During the Civil War some Confederates captured a Yankee soldier near the Steele home. Plans to kill the Union man were made, but as one Confederate soldier raised his rifle to fire it was knocked out of his hand by another comrade and the bullet lodged in a nearby tree. Young Manley Steele, son of William and Lucinda spent the following day trying to dig out the bullet from its lodging place in a large tree. Children of William and Lucinda Steele were as follows: Manilus (Manley) Richard R., Columbus, Mary M., John Franklin, William A., Ellen and George Thomas.

Marjorie Hair Thornton

Chapter Seven

Cemeteries Along The Wire Road

**Woodmen Of The World monuments. The stones depicting a
large tree trunk were popular around the turn of the century.**

Cemeteries Along The Wire Road

On a warm summer day peace and quiet like a shimmering haze, a promise of things to be, hangs over the deserted cemeteries along the Old Wire Road in the Missouri Ozarks. Many of those who once lived along the road now rest in peace. Time marches on, a hundred years are as one. One monument reads simply, *Mama Is Asleep.*

Many of these old cemeteries had their beginning with a single burial in a field near a family home. Often suitable markers were not available; a pile of field rocks had to suffice. Homemade wooden crosses could not withstand the elements of the weather, these too soon deteriorated. Some of the earliest markers found along the WireRoad are dated in the Civil War years.

Smart Cemetery, stone of cottonwood rock.

106

Many of the older monuments were made of cottonwood rock. Plain and unadorned, their mottled surface bleached by winter winds and the relentless rays of many summer suns, they march row on row like a picket fence. It is almost impossible to read the inscriptions on the flat, board-like surface.

Small monuments, often with a lamb resting on the top, remember children of long ago. Many epitaphs carry the inscription *Budded On Earth To Blossom In Heaven*. In all of the older cemeteries a multitude of these small graves bear harsh, mute testimony of the heart-breaking lack of medical knowledge and facilities in days past.

As pioneer women came to make a new home in a new country, their children were often named in honor of a beloved homeland left behind. Tennessee, a woman's name is sometimes seen on the marker, and Missouri — in honor of the new home — was not uncommon.

Scattered throughout the cemeteries of the Ozark region are the Woodmen Of The World monuments. Woodmen Of The World was a fraternal life insurance company founded in Denver, Colorado, in 1890. This organization had many branches throughout the West. The Women's Circle was a woman's organization affiliated with Woodmen Of The World. Numerous monuments were sold to members of this company. The monuments depict the upright trunk of a stalwart tree. They are

Marker in Smart Cemetery, near Clever.

107

solid and remarkably well preserved considering the dates which range from 1900-1915.

The cemeteries listed are merely an example of hundreds along the Wire Road. Only a small percentage of these are well kept and in use today. Others are barely discernible from the roadways.

Stone in Frazier Chapel Cemetery.

Calton Cemetery

A cemetery which contains some very old graves is Calton, in Barry County, Missouri. Several Civil War veterans are buried there. Many of the stones are illegible and the inscriptions are hard to read.

Two stones with legible inscriptions are those of C. W. Jackson, Co. C., First Arkansas Cavalry, and C. C. Jackson, C. 15th. Missouri Cavalry. It is not known whether the Jacksons were brothers, many times during the Civil War brothers did fight on opposite sides, so it is possible.

A large number of cedar trees in this cemetery are said to have been planted by the widow of a Civil War veteran many years ago.

Delaware Cemetery

The Delaware Cemetery is located in Christian County one mile north of the Old Delaware Trading Post. It is a very old cemetery, well kept and in use today. It is located on the east side of James River and can be reached by Highway 14, west of Nixa.

Steele Cemetery

An interesting story is of a search for the site of burials which occurred more than a century ago. The actual plot of the graves of the persons involved may never be located, markers were found by a diligent search which revealed valuable information.

The old Steele Cemetery is located in Township 26 North, Range 24 West, and Section 2 in Stone County, Missouri. It received its name from the Steele family, prominent farmers in the area and is seldom used at this time.

The William Steele home was southwest of the cemetery near a large spring. Information from the late Curtis Davis, a descendant of the Steele family, places the Wire Road on the west side of the Steele cemetery and home. Others maintain that the Wire Road ran farther east on the opposite side of the road and by still another large spring. Perhaps the road forked there, no doubt that both springs were used during the time of the Civil War when hundreds of soldiers were marching along the old trail.

Fred Mieswinkle, Mt. Vernon, Missouri, local historian has relatives buried in Steele Cemetery. For many years he had searched for the graves of his great-grandparents. He had been told that they were buried near Roundtree Springs, west of Springfield. Traveling to the vicinity he visited with an elderly gentleman who gave him more definite information on the burial site. Stopping at still another home he inquired of a young girl if she knew of any grave sites in the area. She replied, "No, there are no graveyards around here, but there are some rocks with people's names on them out by the well house." "Do you mind if I look at them?" asked Fred. The young lady went with him to look at the stones.

There they were—four grave markers, flush with the ground, face up, near the well house. Here was the marker of Fred's great-great grandmother, Margaret Steele, which he had been unable to find.

The old markers were later moved to the Steele cemetery a short distance from the present road, south of the Christian County line.

OTHER BARRY COUNTY CEMETERIES

There are several cemeteries in Barry County that are located on or near the Wire Road. The first on the Northeast is **Osa** near a church named Hilton, after an early settler.

At Madry soldiers are buried near the Clay Hill School. Clay Hill cemetery is located just north 1 mile as well as the soldiers in an unmarked grave within 1 mile west of the Clay Hill School. In a field behind a barn are located a few stones hidden from view near W highway. Coming on down by Camp Bliss Spring and near McDowell Mill is located a small grave yard.

Then on down Flat Creek near the old Jonas Locke place stones have been removed and alfalfa planted on several unknown graves believed to be Indian and Civil War graves.

The Sparks cemetery is located at the junction of U highway toward Butterfield. From the John Crouch's Stage stop about a mile south will be found the Quaker cemetery behind the Merle's Chapel Church. North of Cassville is located the Pilant cemetery.

Other unknown graves unknown to this writer probably exist.

Cassville the county seat of Barry, County, Missouri

Located on the Road from Springfield to Fayetteville, Arkansas now called Main Street or Old highway 37 where the Wire Road passed through the county.

On October 31, pro-secessionist. Governor Claiborne Fox Jackson, and his rump legislature came to Cassville. After signing Missouri's Act of Secession, he raised the Stars and Bars above Cassville's new brick courthouse and Cassville became the State Capitol of Missouri. The title lasted exactly one week. Orders were given by Major General Sterling Price on November 6, 1861 to move the next day in the direction of Pineville.

Oak Hill cemetery at Cassville and south the Old Stubblefield cemetery overlook the Wire Road from the east. One mile south of Cassville is located McMurtry Spring, and the McCary cemetery on the west. Near Washburn, an Old Keetsville cemetery and south an early Cargile cemetery are abandoned.

The Wire Road leaves highway 37 in a southwesterly direction two miles south of Washburn. One mile farther south on highway 37 is located the Old Pad Roller cemetery now known as King. The Rock Springs cemetery is located near the Rock Springs Church on the Wire road. A cemetery located about 1 mile west of Rock Springs just off the Wire Road to the north is on Anderson land. The Pinch Off cemetery located just north of Potts Hill and the Arkansas line, several unknown are buried.

County Line between Barry CO MO & Benton CO AR

Before entering Arkansas where the Battle of Sugar Creek took place is located Pinch Off cemetery where many unknown soldiers are buried near the Cross Timber Hollow.

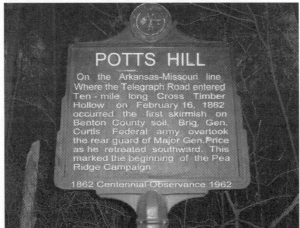

Encampment at Elkhorn Tavern, Pea Ridge, AR 2004

The 15th Missouri Infantry from Claremore, Oklahoma set up their camp near the Tavern, which was used as a hospital in 1862. The Pea Ridge Battle was a very significant battle and a major engagement of the troops of Missouri, Texas & Louisiana and some Indian troops and the loss of several Generals on the battle field. The Battle was fought bravely March 6, 7, 8 of 1862.

Gen. James McBride Camp Sons of Confederate Veterans

McBride Camp honoring the dead at the Confederate Memorial.

The Civil War will stay foremost in many people's mind as their forefathers had been forced into taking action against sometimes there own kinfolk. By the end of the nineteenth century, Northerners were willing to concede that Southerners had fought bravely for a cause they believed just, whereas Southerners with few exceptions were willing to concede that the outcome of the war was probably best for all concerned. There is a flag issue today that should never have happened. Only a few racist people and some politicians try to stir up the feelings of others for votes needed to win an election.

Confederate Memorial near the Elkhorn Tavern

Cross Hollows on the Old Wire Road South of Lowell.

Cross Hollows can be remembered from the Trail of Tears and also the Butterfield Stage route and especially the Civil War where Confederate troops gathered here prior to Pea Ridge.

Fitzgerald's Butterfield Stage Stop in Springdale, Arkansas.

On the Old Wire Road the Fitzgerald's station on Butterfield Overland Mail Route from St. Louis to San Francisco was located. First trip 1858 and last was 1861. Longest and best conducted mail route in the world 2795 miles. Service twice weekly and fare $200.00. Time 25 days and 140 stations for exchange of horses and passengers. (Was written on the marker)

CONFEDERATE CEMETERY AT FAYETTEVILLE

Many unknown soldiers and a few known are buried here from different states from the Pea Ridge & Prairie Grove battles, including General J. Y. Slack removed from the Roller cemetery near Gateway and placed here.

NATIONAL CEMETERY AT FAYETTEVILLE

Many unknown US soldiers from the Civil War are buried here as well as many known.. Many soldiers from all wars are placed here also as their final resting place.
Included are Revolutionary soldiers marked with a granite monument.

Revolutionary Soldiers Remembered with a Granite marker at Fayetteville National Cemetery

From the Bivouac of the Dead
By Theodore O'Hara
The muffled rolls of the sad drums have beat
The soldiers last tattoo;
No more on life's parade shall meet
That brave and fallen few.
On Fame's eternal Camping-Ground
Their silent tents are spread,
And Glory guards, with solemn round
The bivouac of the dead.

Confederate Memorial at Fayetteville, Arkansas

Chapter Eight

Stories, Legends, and Happenings Along The Wire Road

"When the devil comes, it is too late to pray," said Sam Davis

117

Stories, Legends, And Happenings Along The Wire Road

Tell me a story! Grown-ups, as well as children love a good story. Many of the tales recorded in this chapter are stories which have been handed down orally from father to son. Although they have been repeated by word of mouth for many, many years the reader can be assured that nothing has been lost in the telling.

The Alfred Bolin (Bollen) story was hand-written on a school tablet by the granddaughter of Calvin Cloud in 1923. Cloud was murdered by Bolin on October 11, 1862.

The Nellie story written by Mary Scott Hair, local historian, has been told repeatedly in the area where Nellie Johnson boarded a stagecoach bound for California.

Stories of the James brothers, Jesse and Frank, abound in the Missouri Ozarks. The James gang are known to have frequented areas along the Wire Road during their reign of terror in the latter part of the eighteenth century.

The stories in this chapter could have happened anywhere along the Wire Road, or elsewhere. Almost every family has a storehouse of tales, brought out from time to time, enjoyed, and then stored away for future generations

The Sam Davis Story

Posing as soldiers, groups of lawless men committed many vicious crimes during and after the Civil War. On August 29, 1861, shortly after the Battle of Wilson's Creek, several outlaws rode into Galena, Missouri, county seat of Stone County, where they captured John Cox II, his son, James Harrison Cox, Clem Davis, his son Sam Davis, and others. Forcing them to march eight miles to a location on Crane Creek, they spent the night around an open campfire. They later went to the home of William B. Cox, and forced him to march to the place where the others were being guarded.

After breaking camp the next morning, the captured men were made to march without breakfast along the Wire Road to the

McCullah Stop, a distance of three miles. There they were taken up a long, wide valley north of the Trading Post. James and William B. Cox were released because they were so young; the balance of the men were placed under the command of William Shook, who lined them up side by side.

Realizing that they were about to be killed, Clem Davis whispered to his son, telling him to make a break and keep running. Sam Davis, heeding his father's advice, escaped. The others were killed on the spot. Sam Davis ran for his life until he was exhausted, he then hid in the underbrush. After a time he heard someone walking and knew that he was being followed. Groping and finding a large rock Sam waited until he was able to see the person pursuing him. Taking aim, he threw the large stone which found its mark, killing the first man responsible for the death of his father. Sam Davis vowed that he would not rest until all of the outlaws had answered with their lives for the atrocious crime.

Sam Davis escaped and left this area, but he returned periodically. Each time Davis returned to Stone County, Missouri, things happened. There was an accidental drowning; a shoemaker was found with an ax in his skull; there was a man who never left his supper table; and one who never reached his intended destination in Texas.

One of the men sought by Sam Davis was Bill Manning, a resident of Lawrence County. When Sam Davis went to the home of Bill Manning he called him to come to the front door of his home. Bluntly he said, "Bill Manning, I have come to kill you"

Manning answered, "Do I have time to pray?'

"No," said Sam Davis, "When the devil comes, it is too late to pray." It has been said that when Sam Davis died, not one of the men responsible for the death of his father was still living.

A Hanging In Stone County, Missouri

The Civil War was about over; soldiers were going home. The state of Missouri was still under military command.

A small band of thirteen Confederate soldiers came riding through the Crane community making their way southward. Word soon spread through the area; Union Guards were told to report to their captain. The Home Guard could capture and court martial these Confederate soldiers for being traitors to their country and they could be put to death.

Some of the Home Guards didn't want to take part in this action, holding that the War was over and that the men should be left to ride on through and go to their homes. The captain pursued his case and the Home Guard, with some members not participating, captured the Confederates. They were given a court trial for being traitors to the United States, and were convicted and sentenced to be hanged.

The men on their horses were taken up a small hollow some two miles south of Crane. Their hands were tied behind them, a rope was put around their neck, and the horses were led under a tree. The rope was put over the limb of the tree, pulled tight and tied. The horse was slapped hard on the rump to make it jump, and the man was left hanging in the air to die of a broken neck or to strangle to death.

Late in the evening two women walked to the scene to see what the Guards had done to the men. They found that one of the men was not dead, they cut him down and set him free. Later they took the man to their home, put him to bed, and cared for him. After a few days the Confederate soldier recovered enough to travel. The women who rescued him prepared enough food for him to take on his journey home. One night after dark they gave him the food and directions home. The lone soldier disappeared into the night, never to be heard from again.

Author's Note:
This story was written by the late Leonard Williams, teacher and historian. A note at the end of the story states: "Grandfather Williams was in the Home Guard. The story was told to the Williams children with a warning that it was not to be repeated to anyone. The Home Guard split over the incident causing hard feelings in the community for several years."

Jesse James - Saint Or Sinner?

The name of Jesse James is a legend in the Missouri Ozarks. Jesse was born September 5, 1847. He was the son of Robert and Zerelda Cole James, who had migrated from Kentucky to Missouri in 1842. Jesse married a cousin, Zee Mimms.

Jesse James and his brother, Frank, were too young to enlist in the military at the beginning of the Civil War. Frank later enlisted in the Home Guard when he was eighteen years of age. Both Jesse and Frank rode with notorious William Clark Quantrill gang, and also with the "Bloody Bill" Anderson guerrillas. Both Quantrill and Anderson participated in raids in southwest Missouri and northern Arkansas. There are many stories of the James brothers' activities along the Wire Road during, and after the Civil War.

Stories of how Jesse James robbed the rich and gave to the poor still persist even to the present time. Was Jesse James a hero? The truth indicates that he was a ruthless, cold-blooded killer. Other than this he was a very ordinary man. How then did he become a saint in the imagination of the American public? It has been said that the Jesse James portrayed as a legendary hero never lived at all except in the minds of those who wished to believe.

Jesse James was killed at the age of thirty-four years. He was shot in the back by an enemy, Robert Ford, who was eager to collect the reward money.

A marker on the grave of Jesse James reads in part: "Murdered by a traitor and a coward whose name is not worthy to appear here."

Jesse James at Dug Springs

The following story was related by William (Bud) Hair. He was an elderly man and seriously ill at the time, yet he enjoyed telling stories about events which happened when he was a young man.

"When I was a young boy a cousin and I rode our ponies up the Wire Road to Dug (Hodge) Spring on a Sunday afternoon. While we were there a man rode up on a horse. The first thing that drew our attention was the fact that he had a fine, new saddle. At that time every boy in the community dreamed of having a new saddle. The man said that the saddle had rubbed a sore place on the neck of his horse. He asked, ' Would one of you boys like to trade saddles with me?'

"We don't have any money," we replied. We were both thinking of how handsome the new saddle would look on our pony. The man removed the saddle, and replaced it with one belonging to us. Then he rode away. We later learned that he was no other than Jesse James, the notorious outlaw."

Jesse James Gang Robs Entire Town

This story was related to Leaford Gold by a friend, Charlie Burkhart.

Charlie Burkhart lived near Brown's Spring, Missouri. He had a cousin who lived in Butler, and operated a store there. One morning the cousin was preparing to open the store for the day's business when he recognized a man walking down the street; the man was Jesse James. Jesse asked the operator of the store what he was doing, and the man told him he was opening his store. Jesse James told him to go into the store and lock the door of his place of business. He did as he was told; he later learned that every store in the small town was robbed by the Jesse James gang that morning. His store was the only exception.

Childhood Remembrances Of The Wire Road

Evert Lee Hair, Sr., living with his parents on the Wire Road remembered that he and his brothers often stood in the gangway of their father's barn and watched the covered wagons traveling down the Wire Road. Each wagon usually had a chicken coop in the back and a cow tied behind the wagon. Often the children of the large families would be walking, sometimes one or both of the parents would be walking with them. The deep ruts in the dirt road made riding unpleasant.

The Hair brothers once saw four wagons moving slowly down the old road. The lead wagon was pulled by a team of horses, the second and third were pulled by teams of oxen, and the fourth pulled by horses brought up the rear. These were the only oxen Evert ever remembered seeing.

Evert remembered his father telling him of the old log schoolhouse where he attended school three months out of the year. School usually began in July, after crops had been laid by. The school seats were made from split logs which had been smoothed a little. A later Chapel School was the first frame school constructed in Stone County, Missouri.,

Ninety-two children attended Chapel School at one time with two teachers. Almost every family had a large number of children, one family had 21 children; the father had been married twice. Another family had 18 children who all had the same mother. Many young men and women attended school until they were 18 or 20 years old. Evert remembered one young lady who was 25 years old and still attended school. She was said to have been so lazy that she had rather attend school than work on her parent's farm.

The Billings Times
June 21, 1906

Frank and John Hood were tried in the Stone County Circuit Court last week on the charge of killing Charles S. Angus on March 2, last near Hurley, Stone County. Circuit Judge John T. Moore and Prosecuting Attorney Rufe Scott both being related to the Hoods disqualified and Judge Johnson of Pierce City was called to sit in the case while E. M. Hays was appointed special prosecutor.

Relatives of young Angus employed W. P. Sullivan of this city while relatives of Mrs. Angus employed James George of Cassville to assist in the prosecution. The defense was represented by T. L. Viles and George Thornberry of Galena. The case was hotly contested on both sides and lasted the greater part of the week.

It is generally conceded that the state made an exceptionally strong case and it appeared that a long term in the penitentiary was the slightest punishment the defendants could reasonably expect, as there was scarcely a mitigating circumstance in the whole case in their behalf. The jury, after being out some 24 hours, returned a verdict of not guilty about 4 P.M. Sat. afternoon. Much chagrin and disappointment is shown by Angus friends in the vicinity and the expression is freely and openly made that the ends of justice have been far from being reached in the disposition of the case. Perhaps the jurors alone can tell how or why they reached such a verdict.

Women And Children, Orphans Of The Civil War

As troops of the southern Army from the South, and forces of the Federal Army from the North and East, moved into southern Missouri and the Ozarks the Wire Road became the main artery leading from Fayetteville, Arkansas, to Springfield, Missouri. In August, 1861, shortly before the major battle at Wilson's Creek, 12,000 soldiers were said to have camped near the Wire Road on Crane Creek. Food for the men and roughage for the horses were foraged from farmers in the area.

With the husbands and sons away at war, the task of providing for the large families fell to the women and children. The extreme hardships endured by women during the Civil War have never been, and perhaps never will be, recorded.

The early settlers who had only recently come to the Ozarks from Kentucky, Tennessee, Illinois, and other states were already facing the monumental task of providing for their large families. Long, hard hours of back-breaking work were required to provide even the barest necessities of life. Food for the household and roughage for the livestock had, of necessity, to be grown in the spring and summer months and harvested later in the season.

In the winter dugouts and cellars held potatoes, turnips, onions, and other vegetables. Smoke houses were filled with meat; large stone jars held pickles and sauerkraut.

Imagine the heartbreak and desperation of the pioneer mother as he watched the soldiers steal, plunder, and literally snatch food from the mouths of her hungry children. It was not uncommon for entire families to follow the armies hoping to obtain enough food for survival.

Alfred Bolin, Outlaw

Alfred Bolin was born near the small village of Ponce De Leon. Of uncertain parentage, he was abandoned by his mother when very young. For a time, he lived alone until one day he wandered to the home of Calvin and Mary Jane Cloud. The Clouds, with children of their own, opened their home and heart to the homeless boy.

Alfred Bolin was said to have been an obedient child until he was grown. One day he rode off with a group of lawless men and began his life of crime. By his own admission, he killed at least 40 people, most of them children and old men.

The following story was written by Iva Robinson, granddaughter of Calvin and Mary Jane Cloud. Calvin Cloud was murdered by Alfred Bolin. There are many different spellings of the Bolin name. Mrs. Robinson chose to use the Bollen version when she wrote the story in long hand in 1923.

"Alf Bollen's parents died when he was very young. He stayed here and there among strangers. About 12 years of age he came to Calvin Clouds, down on James River, near the McCall bridge. He worked for his board and his clothes, and seemed to enjoy life very much. He was a well-behaved youngster, and obedient, at the beginning of the Civil War. Calvin Cloud joined the Union Army, and Alf joined the Confederate Army. Of course that was the division line between him and the Cloud family. Only just for a short stay he would return, until one day he came back and stayed all day with Jane Cloud and the children. That evening just about sundown, Calvin Cloud came home for something to eat and feed for his horse. As he rode up to the lot gate, he was greeted by Alf with a friendly, 'Hello.' Alf drew his revolver and shot him as he was about to unlatch the gate. Mrs. Cloud, hearing the shot, ran to see. Alf was still there, never trying to escape. She said, 'Alf, you have killed Calvin. I thought you and Calvin were good friends. He has given you a home all these years.'

"Alf said, 'Jane, I think as much of Calvin as I ever did, but I want his rifle.' Alfred helped to carry him to the house and laid him just inside the door on the floor. Alf took his rifle and fled. That was the last the Cloud family heard from him for at least six months.

"There was a large reward for Alf Bollen's capture, dead or alive. Then one evening it was cold and snowing very hard. A man rode up to the gate of the Cloud home and demanded Jane Cloud to appear next morning at Ozark, Missouri, at 9 o'clock for Court. Never told why. So next morning she saddled her horse and rode 30 miles through the wind, the snow and the cold. The snow was a foot deep, and it was only about two months before her last baby was borned (sic).

"Some of Alf's own gang had killed him and beheaded him for the reward and wanted her to come and identify the head. When Mrs. Cloud got to Ozark, they learned she was there at once. They brought the head to her for identification. It was covered with blood, she demanded that the blood be washed off. They did so, and took her in the room to see it. Then she told them that it was really his head, and she was proud to identify it and filled out an affidavit to that effect. They were supposed to return the head to the body, and it and the body were buried not far from Ozark, Missouri, although there were not many buryin' places at that time. Some say his body was not buried at all, only tied to a tree not far from Ozark, Missouri, and left there for the beasts of the land and the fowls of the air to despair (sic).

"Alf Bollen and his gang stole and murdered and robbed quite awhile before his own gang finally got him for the reward. This is a true story, because the Cloud family was my own grandparents."

Iva Robinson, Writer

John R. Kelso

John R. Kelso was a most unusual man, he was ambitious and a distinguished student, formal in manner, precise in speech, and temperate in all things including intoxicating liquor and tobacco.

Kelso attended a special school in Ozark, Missouri, where he formed no friendships and had no companions, holding himself aloof from the student body.

Kelso joined the Dallas County Home Guard at the outbreak of the Civil War. He served as First Lieutenant in the Fourteenth Missouri State Militia, and later transferred to the Eighth Missouri Militia, where he served as Captain of Company M. He approached his military duties with a fanatical zeal and was a leader in the Union Army.

Captain Kelso thought all Confederates were traitors and so were deserving of death. He became a cold-blooded killer, committing murder without cause. In 1870, young John R. Kelso, Jr., committed suicide rather than face his father's wrath after using tobacco, a thing that was strictly prohibited in the Kelso household.

Captain Kelso was elected to Congress in 1864, and tried by any means to thwart the President's efforts toward a rational plan of reconstruction. He will be remembered for his fanatical ideals and for the crimes he committed against his fellow man.

"Nellie"

Eons before author, Zane Gray, wrote his western thriller, *The Lure Of Dim Trails*, both man and beast were probing unknown territory. Which came first—man or beast—is immaterial for both often traveled on the same trails. While travelers today seek out well defined freeways they retain an interest in "how things used to be." May it ever be so.

The summer of 1958 was a busy one; plans that had been in the making for two years were about to take shape. On September 18th of that year the Centennial Celebration of the first run of the Butterfield Overland Mail from Tipton, Missouri, to San Francisco, California, would be re-enacted.

Plans which had been underway for the past two years started to fall into a well organized pattern, soon "The day" arrived. The Overland Mail caravan headed by John Frizzell, an Oklahoma oil man, pulled out of Tipton "right on the dot." Traveling with Mr. Frizzell, who was gathering material for a book, was his wife and

127

their teenage son and daughter. The caravan kept to paved roads and highways, yet followed the old trail whenever possible. Large crowds turned out along the way to welcome the visitors.

It is fun now and then to examine a scrapbook filled with pictures and clippings of the BIG event. Most everyone was/is familiar with the history of the Butterfield Overland Mail; the real purpose of the venture was to carry the mail. However, in order to lower expense, the company also hauled passengers on the long route. Sometimes the stagecoaches were filled to overflowing.

Few people outside of Stone County, Missouri, are aware that the first woman to travel to San Francisco from this area boarded the stagecoach in northern Stone County. She was Nellie Steele Johnson, wife of a Presbyterian minister, the Rev. Thomas Johnson. Her brother was William Steele whose farm in northern Stone County was just off the Butterfield Trail a short distance. As late as 1928, the big log house was a landmark near the Steele Cemetery. Now about all there is left is a heap of stones where three huge fireplaces warmed the big rooms letting warmth seep up through the loft where the boys climbed a crude ladder fastened to the wall to their feather beds and sound sleep. The fireplace rocks and a Japonica bush—for always an old house place is marked by a Japonica bush—were there in 1958.

The Butterfield Stage line cut across the northeast forty the house was located on and traveled toward the Steele house. As it did so, it forked, one angle going near the house, then it rejoined the main trail yon side of the house and a big spring nearby.

In 1958, our local historian, Fred Steele, who was a grandson of the Rev. William Steele, owner of the place, said a well-established road was there for travel at least 16 years before the Butterfield Trail was marked for the carrying of the mail and taking passengers "Out West" in style. Along about 1819, or possibly earlier, surveyors established a route from St. Louis to Paris, Texas, a part of which was this old road across the corner of the Steele farm. Later, one of the Springfield Fulbrights went over the whole route on horseback.

According to Fred Steele, now deceased, the Rev. Johnson left his family in Missouri and traveled to California with a wagon train. At the time there was **little hope** that his wife and four

Nellie Johnson's granddaughter

129

children would be joining him in a couple of years. But preachers then, as now, were led by the Spirit, and that's how come him to go.

It is easy to imagine Nellie Steele Johnson's excitement at the prospect of going by stagecoach all the way to California in about twenty-five days. But it is doubtful if she realized the importance of her place in history, being the first woman to make the trip from Missouri to California, via the Butterfield Stage. And the place where she got on the stage was at the point where the Trail crossed the northeast corner of the Steele's "house forty."

Fred said his great-aunt Nellie made the trip in October, 1858. As was the custom, she visited her relatives 'round and about,' telling them goodbye. And came to her brother William's last for there she knew she could board the stage not far from the house.

The women in the family cooked and fixed up a great basket of food, "grub," it was called then, to take along on the trip. That would be a great saving, for traveling with four children, even today, is not much of a lark and was even less so then, with stations so few and far between. So, the basket was waiting next day.

Some accounts tell of the arrival of the stagecoach, saying it was announced by bugle notes. Fred said he had been told there was ringing of bells or some such sound which could be heard for quite some distance. Anyway, on the day Nellie Johnson and her four children—Margaret who was 16 and the three boys, Finis, John, and William—climbed on board, they had been in such a rush they forgot the basket of homemade goodies! But the Steele children had a feast.

At one point on the way, the stagecoach was stopped by a band of Indians. They asked to see the white children riding on the coach; and when their wish was granted, the coach rolled on its way. Margaret remembered that incident and told about it many times. It was a rugged trip.

But the twenty-five days passed, and the wife and children were greeted by the Rev. Johnson. California became their home state. A fourth son, Jimmie, was born in California.

In 1958, when the Centennial caravan reached San Anselmo, California, Nellie Steele Johnson's granddaughter, Myrtle Johnson Elliott, joined the caravan along with Buck Brown of Yucca Valley. He was a second cousin of **Kit Carson**. They traveled in an ox-drawn covered wagon!

Mary Scott Hair

Ma Barker And Her "Boys"

"You'll have to talk to Ma, she handles the boys." This was the standard answer that George Barker, husband of Arizona Donnia (Ma) Barker gave in reply to anyone who questioned the activities of the four Barker sons. Ma Barker had the misguided opinion that everyone was trying to persecute her "boys", and she defended them through thick and thin. Although she was never arrested for a crime, Ma planned and executed bank and payroll robberies and at one time kidnapped a wealthy St. Paul Brewer, William A. Hamm, Sr., collecting $100,000 for his release.

George and Arizona Donnia (Clark) who were married in Aurora, Missouri, on September 14, 1892, by the Rev. W. B. Cochran, pastor of the First Christian church, obtained the marriage license at the Lawrence County Courthouse, Mt. Vernon, Missouri.

Arizona was born near Ash Grove, Boone Township, Greene County, in 1872. She was the third of four children of Jake and Emiline (Parker) Clark, who were married in Greene County, on December 8, 1864. The father died in the 1870's and the mother then married Reuben Reynolds and had one daughter, Buetta Reynolds.

The family moved to Aurora about 1889. An older daughter, Electra Clark, was married to A. J. Watesburg, also of Aurora. They were married at Mt. Vernon on April 6, 1889.

George Barker, husband of Arrie (Ma) Barker, was thought to have come to Aurora from Lebanon, Missouri, and may have been employed in the mines. The first son of the Barkers, Herman, was born in 1894. Lloyd was born in 1896.

In 1898, George and Ma Barker purchased a lot at 108 Jasper Street, Aurora, and another son, Arthur, was born there in 1899. The Aurora property was sold by the Barkers on September 16, 1899, and they reportedly moved to Christian County near Riverdale. Apparently the Barkers moved often as the last son,

Freddie, was also born in Aurora, where the older sons attended school before moving to Webb City, Missouri.

The four Barker boys seemed to be prone to trouble with the local police wherever they went. Arthur (Doc) stole a government car in 1918, he later was tried and sent to the Oklahoma State Penitentiary for the murder of a Tulsa night watchman. Ma said he was innocent; he was paroled in 1932.

Lloyd Barker robbed a Kansas bank in 1922, and was sent to Leavenworth prison for twenty-five years. Herman robbed several banks and after killing a policeman, committed suicide. Ma insisted that it was a police execution. Fred was arrested for robbing a bank in Winfield, Kansas; he was paroled in 1931. Doc was sent to Alcatraz prison for the kidnapping of a wealthy Minneapolis, Minnesota banker. He received a life sentence.

With the police hot on their trail, Ma, who had masterminded a plot, and son Freddie fled to Oklawaha, Florida, where both were killed in a forty-five minute shoot-out with the F.B.I. agents on January 16, 1935. Arthur (Doc) was killed trying to escape Alcatraz prison in 1939. The father, George Barker, died in February 1941, and the last surviving member of the family, Lloyd, moved to Colorado where he was killed by his wife in 1949.

Thus, with the exception of father George, all members of the Barker family, sometimes called the Bloody Barkers, met an untimely end. All of the family except Lloyd, are buried in the Williams Timberhill Cemetery between Welch and Miami, Oklahoma. Stones placed side by side bear the following inscriptions:

Herman: October 30, 1893—August 29, 1927

Kate: Died January 16, 1935—October, 1935. (Evidently the second date is the date of interment in the Oklahoma Cemetery as both Kate, "Ma" and son, Fred, were moved there from Florida, their original burial site.)

Arthur: 1939

George: February, 1941

Apparently Lloyd, who was killed in Colorado is the only member of the family who was not buried on the wind-swept prairie of the Williams Timberhill Cemetery.

Bushwhackers

During the Civil War, a band of 120 Arkansas Bushwhackers came up the old Wilderness Road into Stone County, Missouri, on a foraging expedition. Here they met Ali Baker, a young, law-abiding man, who opposed them. They killed him and rounded up 150 cattle and what plunder they could carry. Then they camped for the night preparing for an early start for Arkansas the next day. But while they were rounding up the cattle, the Captain of the Stone County guards was rounding up his faithful band at Galena. At midnight they surrounded the Bushwhackers and killed all but 20 who escaped back into Arkansas.

The citizens of the county were largely composed of home-loving and home-protecting descendants of Scotch-Irish heritage from Kentucky and Tennessee.

Ref: Stone County Booklet, 1927.

The Young Massacre
1932

Many years after the Battle of Wilson's Creek, a tragic event took place at the home of Mrs. Willie Young, near Brookline, Missouri. The home was located near Little York, a place made familiar by history of the Civil War.

The body of Marshal Noe, a Republic resident, had been found in a roadside ditch by Lillard Hendrix, brother of Greene County Sheriff Marcell Hendrix. Harry Young, son of Willie Young, was wanted for questioning. Officers had suspected that Harry Young, and his brother Jennings, might be operating a stolen car ring. Vanita Young and Lorena Conley Young, sisters of Harry and Jennings Young had been seen driving a number of flashy cars with out-of-state licenses in the area. Some bore Texas plates; Lorena lived in Houston, Texas.

Late in the afternoon of January 2, 1932, officers raided the farm home where the brothers were reported to have been seen. They suspected that the pair would be armed as they were considered dangerous.

Driving up to the farm home, officers called for the brothers to come out. There was no answer and it was thought for a time that they might have escaped. Sheriff Marcell Hendrix told his officers that there was only one way to find out; that was to rush the place. This proved to be an unwise decision for the three officers, Sheriff Marcell Hendrix, Deputy Sheriff Wiley Mashburn and Detective Frank Pike. As they pushed against the door it yielded—and flew open. The men were met by a blast of bullets and Sheriff Marcell Hendrix fell, mortally wounded. Deputy Sheriff Wiley Mashburn, although fatally wounded lived until he reached a Springfield hospital; Frank Pike was also wounded. Deputy Sheriff, Ollie Crosswhite, was shot between the eyes. Viewing the body after it was brought back to Springfield, a brother of Crosswhite told of a dream he had some time before in which his brother was fatally wounded by a bullet to the forehead. "See the hole between his eyes? It is just as I dreamed," he said. Also killed were Tony Oliver, Springfield Chief of Detectives, Sidney Meadows, Police Officer, and Charlie Houser, Police Officer. Officers who escaped were Detective Frank Pike, Detective Owen Brown and Motorcycle Policeman Virgil Johnson.

The Young brothers managed to escape in the aftermath of the murders of the six police officers. After a time their trial led to Houston, Texas, where it was found that the two had rented a room telling the owner that one of the men had some teeth extracted and must be quiet for a few days.

When Texas officers converged on the place where the Young brothers were hiding, they heard shots. Rushing the door where Harry and Jennings Young were taking refuge, they found the brothers sitting on the floor, facing one another. Jennings Young was dead and Harry was unconscious having been wounded twice in the chest. He was rushed to a Houston, Texas, hospital where he died shortly. The Young Massacre is thought to have been the largest number of police officers slain at one time in the nation.

Indian Annie Tames Unruly Boy
As told by Evert L. Hair, Sr.

Many years ago the family of Mr. and Mrs. Jim DeWitt lived in the small village of Boaz, in Christian County, Missouri. Their home was across the road from the general store, scene of much activity as farmers came on Saturday to buy their week's supply of groceries. Mrs. DeWitt was seriously ill and the chores of cooking, laundry, and housework fell to the DeWitt children of the large family. The oldest daughter, twelve years old, tried to care for her ailing mother and the younger brothers and sisters. The father worked long, hard hours in the fields to provide for his wife and large brood of children.

The DeWitts had only one son. He was a very unruly child who pestered his sisters as they tried to do their mother's work. The father was working in the field one day when one of the small daughters ran to him, crying. She told her father that she and her sisters were unable to prepare the noon meal because her brother was so naughty. As the girls sat at the dining table hulling peas for the noon meal, the brother sneaked underneath the table and tried to hack their bare toes with a large butcher knife.

Mr. DeWitt, hot, tired, and troubled by this latest turn of events, unhooked his plow and drove to the general store in Boaz. There he bought two chains and two padlocks. Proceeding on home he placed one chain around his son's ankle and the other around his wrist and tossed him in the nearby corncrib.

Indian Annie, who had been found on the Trail of Tears as an infant, also lived in Boaz. She heard the father talking about the naughty, unruly boy and his desire to find a housekeeper. She offered her services on one condition, that she be allowed to discipline the DeWitt son at her own discretion. Overjoyed to be relieved of some of his responsibilities, DeWitt hired Annie on the spot. Beginning her duties at the home, she ordered the son to go to the well for a bucket of water.

In his usual arrogant manner the son replied, "Go get it yourself," and then ran away. He had not reckoned with the common knowledge that Annie was a full-blooded Indian and could run like a deer. In no time at all she caught the boy and held him fast in her powerful grip. It certainly came as a surprise to the troublesome boy that someone could make him—and would make him—mind. Realizing Annie's authority over him, it is said that he became her willing slave.

Chapter Nine

Life In The Ozarks

Life In The Ozarks

The years passed. The Civil War drew to a close in the year of 1864. Memories of the destruction, death, and suffering endured did not vanish from the Ozarks region overnight. Only time, the healer of all wounds, could bring solace, erase the scars, and restore a semblance of law and order to a torn and bleeding countryside.

The Wire Road, from Ft. Smith, Arkansas, to St. Louis, Missouri, was a much traveled thoroughfare during this period of time. Supplies from the isolated country stores were often freighted by wagon and team from the larger cities. After the coming of the railroads, supplies were hauled from the nearest railroad town.

Dealers in cattle, sheep, hogs, turkeys, etc., herded their droves up the Wire Road to the larger markets. Traveling from Arkansas, they crossed the White River on the Kimberling Ferry which forded the river at the point where Kimberling City now stands. Proceeding on to Springfield, cattle and other products of the farm were shipped to St. Louis, Kansas City, and other larger markets. The Wire Road and the old Wilderness Road located farther east were two of the major arteries from Arkansas to Springfield, and beyond, near the turn of the century.

Life in the Ozarks continued on at a leisurely pace. Children were born, grew to man and womanhood and, in turn, brought forth children of their own. Many pioneers of the Ozarks were born, lived their lives, and died on a tract of land homesteaded by their parents or grandparents. Often the land had been obtained from the government as a grant for military service (See stories in Chapter Six.)

Early settlers of the area clung to the old traditions and superstitions. The dialect and customs of the area still set the Missouri-Arkansas Ozarks apart from other areas of the country. The average resident of the Ozark hills is an individual of integrity, high morals, and respectability. True, a few families living below the accepted poverty level do accept charity. Most are fiercely independent, as were their fathers before them. They disdain anything that smacks of a government hand-out and are quick to tell the world that they are not beholden to anyone. And they seldom are!

Large families were the rule, rather than the exception, in past generations. It was not uncommon for parents to have eight or ten children. Children's games were a part of every day living before the advent of television. Riddles, old sayings, weather predictions, home remedies, good and bad luck omens were all a part of the woof and warp of the Ozarkian way of life. Customs are still passed down from father to son. Seldom are they written, or recorded, in any manner.

The purpose of writing this book of the happenings along the Wire Road has been to preserve its history for future generations. The same is true of the customs of the area.

Remedies Of The Past

Headache cure: If you sleep with a pair of scissors under your pillow at night your headache will be gone by the following morning.

Crick in the neck: Find a hog pen close by where the hog has rubbed its neck on the fence. Rub your neck on the same spot, within minutes the crick should be gone.

Stomach ache: Cut off some hair behind your left ear. Place the hair in your right hand and toss it over the left shoulder.

Sty on the eye: Have you been telling the truth? Remember, lies cause sties.

Sunburn: Apply thick laundry starch directly to the damaged skin and let dry. Repeat as often as necessary.

Cough and sore throat: Get some onions from last year's garden and bake them in the oven until tender. Pour the juice off in a glass, let cool and drink.

Toothache: Burn a piece of paper on an old plate, take a wad of cotton and wipe the brown sweat from the plate and plug it in the tooth.

Cold sores: Wash mouth frequently with some tea, or vinegar and water; also drink freely of sarsaparilla tea.

Bee stings or insect bites: Make a paste of common earth dirt and water and place over the bite. Cover with cloth and let dry. Placing a cud of tobacco which has been chewed on the sting has been found to be helpful. It will draw out the poison.

To prevent measles: Tie a bag of asafetida around the neck.

To stop nose bleeds: Cut a piece of salt pork the size of your nostril, insert the plug and leave until bleeding stops.

Burns: Rub with a banana, corn starch, or vanilla.

Cuts: Place the membrane lining of an egg shell over the wound to stop bleeding.

Stomach trouble: Make a tea of white oak bark and drink.

To cure boils: Prepare a slippery elm poultice and place on the boil, or crush the leaves of the maderia plant and place on the boil.

Wart cure: Steal your best friend's dirty dish rag, rub the warts, and bury the rag. When the dish rag rots the warts will be gone. Or go to a house where there is an orchard, steal a knife from the house. Go to a fruit tree and cut as many notches as you have warts, go away and the warts will leave. Or take three grains of corn and go to a place where the road forks three ways, put a grain of corn in each road and put a rock on top of the corn. The warts will leave you and go to the person knocking the rocks off the corn.

Cramps in the stomach: Red pepper tea will cure the cramps, drink as hot as you can stand it.

Influenza or lumbago: Take equal parts of honey, lemon juice and whiskey. Mix and drink. Or mix milk, honey, butter and garlic, and drink.

Leg cramps: Place the toe of one shoe inside the other when you go to bed.

Ringworm: Take a teakettle of boiling water, rub your fingers in a circle the size of the ringworm on the inside of the lid and then around the ringworm. Do the same with the forefinger, then with the thumb again. Do this alternately with all the fingers and thumb on that hand. Leave and don't look back, the ringworm will go away.

Asthma: Red pepper, six or seven pods, middle size handful of black pepper, a handful of cloves, a handful of cinnamon bark, some anise seed, a handful of mustard seed and a cup of sugar. Put the above in one gallon of water and cook it good. Strain, and put the liquid in a bottle. Dose: three teaspoons of the liquid in one-half cup of water twice a day, morning and at bedtime. If you use it full strength for three months you will be well. It will do you no harm, use it as often as you can stand it. Another remedy for asthma: dissolve five cents worth of salt peter in a pint of water and saturate two quarts of dry pulverized jimsonweeds; then dry in oven and inhale with a pipe or a coal of fire. People who suffer from asthma should eat plenty of carrots.

Asthma or croup: To one-half pint of strong cider vinegar add one tablespoon of salt. Swallow one-half a spoonful every ten seconds. This will generally give relief within one minute.

Rheumatism: Carry a buckeye or a potato in your pocket.

Nose bleeds: Drop as many drops of blood as you are years old in a bottle and cork the bottle tight, hang in a chimney. Your nose will never bleed again as long as the bottle hangs there.

Nail in foot: If you stick a nail in your foot, pull it out. Stick a piece of tallow in the wound as far as the nail went, it will heal right

141

away.

Old 'Sayings'

To cross the broom and mop will keep the witches out.

When it snows big flakes, old Mother Goose is picking her geese.

If you drop a spoon, company will come soon.

Stump your toe, kiss your thumb, you will see your beau before daylight comes.

Rock a cradle empty, babies will be a-plenty.

Dreams at night are the devil's delight, dreams in the morning are the angel's warning.

Dream of fruit out of season, you'll be angry without reason.

Use it up, wear it out, make it do, or do without.

Dimple in the chin, devil within.

Birds of a feather flock together.

It's always darkest just before the dawn.

Pretty is as pretty does.

The first place to look for a helping hand is on the end of your arm.

Early to bed and early to rise makes a man healthy, wealthy and wise.

If a task is worth doing, it is worth doing well.

Independent as a hog on ice—totally independent.

Two heads are better than one, if one is a goat's head.

You can't put an old head on young shoulders.

It's a long road that has no turning.

Sow the wind and reap the whirlwind.

Don't count your chickens before they are hatched.

Spare the rod and spoil the child.

All work makes Jack a dull boy.

Not knowing them from Adam's off ox.

A stitch in time saves nine.

It will never be noticed on a galloping horse.

Don't make a mountain out of a mole hill.

Don't look a gift horse in the mouth.

Don't get hot under your collar - or flip your wig.

Dyed in the wool - and a yard wide - the best.

It's snowing down south; meaning your petticoat is showing.

More trouble than he could say grace over.

Some folks' stories need to be taken with a grain of salt.

Straight from the horse's mouth - from a reliable source.

To sleep tight - ropes were used in the olden days to hold the bed together, a key was used to tighten the rope. Hence the ditty: Sleep tight, don't let the bed bugs bite."

To get down to brass tacks - come to the point.

The wheel that squeaks the loudest gets the grease.

His elevator don't go all the way to the top - he's not playing with a full deck - he doesn't have all his eggs in one basket.

"You scratch my back; I'll scratch yours." Advice often heeded by local politicians.

Top man on the totem pole.

Feeling as fine as frog hair - and it split!

He is so ugly he has to slip up on the dipper to get a drink.

Old 'Sayings'
Similes often used in the Missouri Ozarks

Green as grass	Quiet as a mouse
Crazy as a loon	Gentle as a lamb
Ugly as a mud fence	Keen as a briar
Red as a beet	Cold as a wedge
Pretty as a picture	Mean as a snake
Odd as a $2.00 bill	Drunk as a skunk
Cross as a bear	Sharp as a razor
Cute as a bug's ear	Proud as a peacock
Honest as the day is long	Rough as a cob
Crooked as a rail fence	Happy as a lark
Old as Methuselah	Blue as indigo
Dark as a stack of black cats	Quick as lightning
Cool as a cucumber	Busy as a beaver
Hot as a little red wagon	Poor as Job's turkey
Mad as a hornet	Dumb as an ox

Bold as brass
Meek as a lamb
Sharp as a tack
Fat as a pig
Crooked as a barrel of snakes
Blind as a bat
Dead as a mackerel (herring)
Thick as pea soup
Busy as a cranberry merchant

Slow as the seven year itch
Green as a gourd
Straight as a string
Fit as a fiddle
Deaf as a door knob
High as a kite
Limp as a dish rag
Poor as a church mouse
Stubborn as a mule

Down Memory Lane

All of the following practices were common in the Missouri Ozarks. Do you remember when:

Not every family had a buggy or surrey? Wagons were used for transportation as well as for the farm chores. Straw was placed in the wagon bed, children usually rode in the back while the parents rode on the spring seat in the front.

Telephone lines were maintained by the parties using the line? It was a common practice for anyone to listen in on the conversation if they wished to do so. News of anything unusual, as a fire or emergency of any kind, was spread rapidly by the use of the telephone.

Pie suppers were common, especially at the country schools? Boxes which held the pies were veritable works of art. The school marm's pie often brought a pretty penny as local boys vied for the privilege of eating with her.

You were elated when your parents purchased a Dazey churn? The old stone churn with a wooden paddle soon was obsolete.

Gathering eggs seemed to be so much fun? You were reminded to watch for snakes in the nest, and also for the old "setting" hen whose peck could take a hunk of flesh from your hand or arm.

145

You watched your mother's old turkey hen hide her nest? This was fun, if her eggs were not disturbed she would hatch out the tiny, fluffy turkey (chicks) poults.

You ironed with a sad iron that had to be heated on a wood stove? The early sad irons were made with an attached handle. Later models, which were issued in sets of three, had a detachable wooden handle. An improvement to both of the above models was a gasoline iron that burned a special white gasoline. This type did not prove to be popular as many housewives were afraid of the fuel.

In the Spring you set the incubator, turned the eggs religiously, and could hardly wait to see the baby chicks piping their shell? The brooder house was made ready by placing fresh straw on the floor. A brooder stove, fueled with kerosene kept the small chicks warm. You set the alarm clock, climbed sleepily out of bed for a week or so to go to the brooder house in the middle of the night, checking on the stove and the chicks.

You slept crosswise on a bed with cousins of all ages? Large families made it almost impossible to have a separate bed. Often relatives traveled many miles, it was not at all uncommon to have overnight guests.

Butchering day dawned clear and cold? The crack of a rifle rang out as the cloud-like steam rose upward from the scalding vat. After the hog had been killed the jugular vein in the neck was severed with a sharp knife, skin near the feet were slit and the animal was hung upside down to bleed. Fresh liver from the newly butchered hog was almost invariably served for the noon meal. The first day of butchering hogs was tiring, the second was more so as sausage had to be made, lard ground and rendered. The meat had to be quartered into hams, shoulders, bacon, backbone, ribs, tenderloin, and made ready to be cured. Salt alone was used in the early cure. Later, a sugar cure gave the finished product an improved flavor.

Harvest time was a very busy time? In addition to cooking for the threshing crews, there was the chore of filling the straw ticks with the new, sweet -smelling straw. With a feather bed on top, the straw beds served a real purpose in the unheated houses of the early settlers.

Water was drawn from the well by a pulley with a long rope tied to a metal bucket? Later, the hand pump was invented, still later gasoline engines were used with the pump.

The Saturday night bath was taken in the old galvanized wash tub? Water was at a premium, not because of the scarcity of water, but because of the labor involved in pumping it from the well and carrying it to the farm house. It was not uncommon, at bedtime, for several children to be washed in the same tub of water and with a common wash cloth. Do you remember a separate cloth called the "foot rag?" If you were lucky, you could get by with washing your feet.

You smoothed your feather bed with a broom handle? Snow white sheets were sometimes used as bedspreads. A separate strip of cloth was sewn at the top of the quilts to keep them clean. Washing quilts and bedding was a major problem for the housewife of long ago.

Children often walked two, or three, miles to school the year around? Lunches were sometimes packed in syrup, or lard, buckets. Later, when government commodities came along, lunches were cooked at the schools. For some children, this was the best and most nutritious meal of the day.

When babies wore belly bands? The new mother spent at least nine days in bed so everything would go back in place.

Crackers came in a long, oblong, wooden case that resembled an egg case? A helping of cheese and crackers sold for a nickel or dime at the country store.

Imitation butter was called oleo margarine? A red pill had to be squeezed into the white oleo for coloring.

Company came unexpectedly and you caught a frying chicken, scalded it, picked the feathers off, singed the down over an open fire, cut it up, and fried it before dinner could be served?

You used a cream separator? What a chore it was to wash all the pieces!

Cars came with running boards and isinglass curtains? Most of the fasteners wouldn't work when you wanted to get them on in a hurry.

Dogs had running fits? People were afraid they might be mad, yet a dose of worm medicine would usually fix everything.

You ate corn meal mush for supper, and ate the sliced leftover mush which had been fried the following morning?

Homes for the elderly were unheard of? Children cared for their parents in their own home as a matter of course.

Almost everyone had a large family? The older children dressed and helped care for their younger brothers and sisters.

Pink glass dishes came from the oatmeal boxes? Sometimes the colored glass was given as a premium at the movie or at the local service station.

Outdoor theaters projected movies on a large screen? The current movie showing was often a serial that left the hero or heroine in a precarious position to insure attendance the following week.

The lady of the house sealed her canning jars with sealing wax? This was before jars were sealed with a canning rubber and a zinc lid. The rubbers were also used with glass lids which had a wire bail to hold the lid tight.

You jumped into bed in an unheated room and found that your mother had placed a heated flat iron between the covers to keep you warm?

The outside toilet held a catalogue from either Sears Roebuck and Company or Montgomery Ward?

Your mother made homemade "light" bread, and you were given a piece hot from the oven? Good country butter that had been cooled in the spring house made it even better.

You had "Sunday" clothes that you didn't wear except on special occasions? Dresses and shirts were starched with a mixture of flour and boiling water.

You tied the bluing ball in a small cloth to use over and over on wash day? Later bluing came in a liquid and was easier to distribute evenly in the water.

Floors were mostly covered with linoleum and could be polished with a mixture of melted paraffin and kerosene?

You canned vegetables, fruits, jams, jellies, pickles, and everything you could get your hands on? Sometimes these were not used during the summer months but were put aside for the winter.

Babies had a clean bib for every meal? Their mothers wore an apron to save on washing?

You wore overshoes to school? The mud was sometimes so bad that you could hardly pull your feet from the road.

You picked potato bugs from the plants and dropped them in a can of kerosene? Potatoes had to be planted with the "eyes" up and you wondered if they needed to see how to come from the ground.

Shoes for the entire family were half-soled with leather by the use of an iron shoe last? The foot pieces came in sizes to fit everyone. Excess leather which overlapped on the outside of the shoe was trimmed with a shoe trimming knife.

149

Loose hair which was left in the comb or brush was saved for a "rat?" When placed on the head and covered with hair the "rat" gave an illusion of a fluffy pompadour.

A bad cold was treated by rubbing the chest with skunk, goose, or opossum grease? Then a wool flannel cloth was placed over the grease. Onions were also fried in grease and a poultice was made to place on the chest.

Men had a long mustache? Bits of food accumulated on the mustache, making it a rather unsavory sight at the dining table.

Medicine shows came to town, usually in the spring? The concoctions they sold as medicine often contained a large percentage of alcohol.

The local, annual picnic was the highlight of the year? People came from near and far to meet with their neighbors and friends. Lunch was spread on the ground at the noon meal.

How good the hamburgers tasted at the annual picnic? And how good the popcorn smelled?

Milk for your morning bowl of hot oatmeal was placed on the table in a milk pitcher? Sometimes it may have held pure cream. Glass jugs and paper cartons replaced the milk pitcher How long has it been since you saw a set of dishes which contained a milk pitcher?

The latest style in a hair-do was a spit curl on your forehead?

Yo-yo pillows were the rage?

Doorstops were made of last year's Sears Roebuck catalogue?

The Ouija Board, patented in 1892?

The fad of swallowing gold fish? One man swallowed 24 fish

chased down with orange juice to win a bet. Another swallowed 42 fish in 52 minutes.

Flag pole sitting? Tree sitting? Marathon dancing? A rocking chair contest?

Chain letters, 1935, promising a return of $1,162.50 for only a dime?

Good and Bad Luck Omens

Good Luck:

Carry the left hind foot of a rabbit in your pocket.

Eat blackeye peas on New Years Day. Place a dime under your plate.

Finding a four leaf clover is good luck.

Bad Luck:

A Lone Star quilt is bad luck.

If you iron your husband's shirt tail crosswise he will be cross and grumpy.

You will have bad luck if you stand crosswise on the floor boards.

Walking under a ladder is bad luck.

Mirrors in the home must be covered when a member dies. Otherwise, the next person who looks in the mirror will be the next to die.

Sneeze on Monday for good health
Sneeze on Tuesday for wealth
Sneeze on Wednesday for woe
Sneeze on Thursday, a-traveling you will go.
Sneeze on Friday for sorrow
Sneeze on Saturday, you will see your beau tomorrow
Sneeze on Sunday, you will see the devil the rest of the week.

Definitions

To pull up stakes — leave.

She'll get her come-uppance — what is due her.

Wouldn't that cork you? — dumfound you.

The spittin' image — identical.

Like two turtle doves — close.

A ring tail tooter — a rounder.

He is so ornery — mean.

He got the cart before the horse — not in order.

He could eat 'till the cows come home — a long time.

He felt a little dauncy — light headed.

I'm a mite queasy—rather faint.

I am still juberous of that man — afraid.

He's my sweet patootie — sweetheart.

This dough is all guamed up — a sticky mess.

I feel right tolerable — about average.

Get on your riggin', we're a-goin' to town. — clothes.

Poor man, he's on his last legs — about dead.

Oh, I hurt my tickle bone — elbow.

I tell you that boy is a cutter — rowdy.

That child has lots of play purties — toys.

Her old man came home a faunchin' — raising a ruckus.

I don't want to be beholden to you — owe you.

Bring me a poke to put my duds in — a sack to put my clothes in.

That girl is a yard long and a mile wide — a fine person.

I'm tired of that tom-foolery — trickery.

He was feeling his oats — feeling great.

He ran it in the ground and twisted its tail — carried it too far.

Knee high to a grasshopper — very small.

That was sure a water haul — unproductive.

We kill our own snakes — take care of our own troubles.

We paddle our own canoes — handle our own affairs.

Don't go home in the heat of the day without your blanket — don't go away angry unless you know you are in the right.

She sure drowned the miller — **put too** much milk for the amount of flour used.

Stop that pussy-footing around — slipping around.

If you dilly-dally around you will never get the job done — procrastinate.

It's time to rid up the table — clear off the table.

Riddles

Riddles were a favorite pastime for a rainy day or a long, cold winter evening. Some of the following riddles are very old.

I have a little sister, they call her "Peep-Peep." She wades the waters deep-deep-deep.
She climbs the mountains high-high-high.
Poor little creature, she has but one eye.
Answer: A star.

I'm a strange contradiction, I'm new and I'm old,
I'm often in tatters and oft decked in gold.
Though I never could read, lettered I'm found,
Though loose, I'm bound.
I am always in black, and I'm always in white;
I'm grave and I'm gay, I am heavy and light.
In form too, I differ - I'm thick and I'm thin,
I've no flesh and no bones, yet I'm covered with skin;
I've more points than the compass, more stops than the flute;
I sing without voice, without speaking confute.
I'm English, I'm German, I'm French and I'm Dutch;
Some love me too fondly, some slight me too much;
I often die soon, though I sometimes live ages,
And no monarch alive has no many pages.
                                                    By Hannah Moore
Answer: A book.

154

Two legs sat upon three legs
With one leg in his lap;
In comes four legs, runs away with one leg.
Up jumps two legs, catches up three legs,
Throws it after four legs, and makes him bring back one leg.
Answer: One leg is a leg of mutton, two legs is a man, three legs is
a stool, four legs is a dog.

Arthur O'Bower has broken his band
He comes roaring up the land.
The King of Scots with all his power
Cannot turn Arthur of the Bower.
Answer: A storm of wind.

Long legs, crooked thighs,
Little head, and no eyes.
Answer: A pair of tongs.

Flower of England, fruit of Spain
Met together in a shower of rain;
Put in a bag, tied with a string,
If you'll tell me this riddle, I'll give you a ring.
Answer: A plum pudding.

Little Nancy Etticote, in a white petticoat,
With a red nose;
The longer she stands; the shorter she grows.
Answer: A candle.

Old Mother Twitchitt has but one eye
And a long tail which she lets fly
Every time she goes through a gap
She leaves a bit of her tail in the trap.
Answer: A needle and thread.

Thirty white horses upon a red hill
Now they tramp, now they champ, now they stand still.
Answer: Teeth.

A stick in his hand
A stone in his throat
If you will answer this riddle
I'll give you a groat.
Answer: A cherry.

What has eighteen legs and catches flies?
Answer: A baseball team.

What has a tongue and can't talk?
Answer: A wagon - a shoe.

What has feet but can't walk?
Answer: A yardstick.

What has an eye but can't see?
A needle.

As I was walking to St. Ives I met a man with seven wives,
Seven wives had seven sacks, seven sacks had seven cats,
Seven cats had seven kits,
Kits, cats, sacks and wives, how many were walking to St. Ives?
Answer: One, I was walking to St. Ives.

Big at the bottom little at the top,
Thing in the middle goes flippety flop.
Answer: A churn.

There is the railroad, there are the cars.
Can you spell that without any "R's?"
Answer: THAT.

High as a house, low as a mouse,
Bitter as gall, good after all.
Answer: A walnut.

Round as a biscuit, busy as a bee, Prettiest little thing you ever did
see.

Answer: A watch.

Round as a biscuit, sharp as an awl,
Stick it in your foot, it will make you squall.
Answer: A cocklebur.

Why is the end of a dog's tail like the heart of a tree?
Answer: Because it is farthest from its bark.

Why is a stick of candy like a horse?
Answer: The more you lick it, the faster it goes.

What travels over hills and hollows in the day and rests under the
bed at night?
Answer: Wagon wheels

Weather Predictions and Superstitions

When the wind is in the East
'Tis neither good for man or beast.
When the wind is in the North
The skillful fisher goes not forth.
When the wind is in the South
It blows the bait in the fishes' mouth.
When the wind is in the West
'Tis then it's at its very best.

When the dew is on the grass
Rain will never come to pass.

Rainbow in the morning, sailors take warning
Rainbow at night, sailors delight.

If it rains before seven it will stop before eleven.

Crow on the fence, rain will go hence
Crow on the ground, rain will come down.

When the peafowl loudly calls
Look out for rain and squalls.

If a rooster crows when he goes to bed
He will wake up with rain on his head.

If a cow tries to scratch her ear
It means a shower is very near
When she thumps her ribs with her tail
Look out for thunder, lightning, and hail.

It is widely believed that rain on Easter foretells rain for the next seven Sundays.

It will be a hard winter if the corn husks are so thick you can't find the corn inside.

If the woolly worms are wearing thick, heavy coats, it will be a hard winter.

Hogs predict cold weather by gathering sticks in their mouth to make a bed.

If the first day of the New Year is calm, it will be a dry summer.

A mild Christmas Day is said to be a harbinger of a bountiful harvest.

If it thunders in February there will be a frost on the same day in May.

If the ground hog comes out of his shelter and sees his shadow on February second (or fourteenth, take your pick) he will go back in his hole and there will be six more weeks of winter weather.

Old Games

"It is a happy talent to know how to play."

Ralph Waldo Emerson Journals - 1834

Fox and Goose (Hounds)
Blindman's Bluff
Workup (Scrub)
Ante-over
Ring Around The Rosie
Jacks
Crack The Whip
Shinny
Go In and Out the Window

London Bridge
Hide The Thimble
Hide and Seek
Marbles
Mumble-the-Peg
Cross Out
Two-Eyed Cat
Dare Base
Last Couple Out
King Of The Hill
Soft Ball
Jump The Rope
Heavy, Heavy Hangs Over Your Head
Charades (New Orleans)
Clap In - Clap Out
Blindfold
Pin The Tail On The Donkey
Red Light - Green Light
Rotten Egg
Gossip
Grandma Sissy Saw Died
Spin The Plate

Streets and Alleys
Flying Dutchman
Miller Boy
Farmer In The Dell
Trades
Hangman
Who - What - Where
Post Office
Drop the
    Handkerchief
Three Deep
Boxes
Cat and Mouse
Go To Mill
Tit Tat Toe
Stink Base
Hop Scotch
Tag
Statue
Club Fist
Musical Chairs
Build The Bridge
I Sail My Ship
Soakum
Follow The Leader
Spin The Bottle
May I?
Run, Sheepie Run
Dodge Ball
Slaughter Ball
Simon Says
Telephone

Although dancing was frowned upon in many areas, play parties and kissing games were permissible. Participants in play parties many times executed the same steps to a particular tune without benefit of music. When the Victrola came into use some parents permitted this type of music, but often dancing to any type of music, especially that of the violin or fiddle, was strictly prohibited and considered to be the work of the devil. The same was true of cards; many parents would not allow their offspring to use playing cards but sanctioned dominoes and checkers.

The following play party game was best executed by musical accompaniment. The various actions were carried out until the song was finished.

Marching Around The Levee:

We're marching round the levee, we're marching round the levee
We're marching round the levee, for we have gained the day.

Go in and out the window, go in and out the window
Go in and out the window for we have gained the day.

Go forth and face your lover, go forth and face your lover
Go forth and face your lover, for we have gained the day.

I measure my love to show you, I measure my love to show you
I measure my love to show you, for we have gained the day.

I kneel because I love you, I kneel because I love you
I kneel because I love you, for we have gained the day.

One kiss before I leave you, one kiss before I leave you
One kiss before I leave you, for we have gained the day.

Telephone:

Players sit in a circle. One player is designated to give the message, whispering it to the next player on the right. This continues until all players have received and transmitted the message. The last player repeats the message as he understands it. Seldom does it resemble the original message.

Twenty Questions:

The object of this game is to identify an object by asking a few questions as possible. A limit of twenty questions may be asked. The player who guesses the subject is the winner.

Run, Sheepie, Run:

This is an old, old game similar to Hide and Seek. The player who is "IT" hides his eyes and calls out, "Run, sheepie, run." The other players run and hide while the person who is "IT" counts to a certain number, usually one hundred. Sometimes when the one who had counted was ready to seek out the others he might call out, "A bottle of whiskey, a bottle of rum, all eyes open, here I come." Or he might say, "A bushel of wheat, a bushel of clover, all not hid can't hide over." The object of the game was to reach home base or get in "free." When a player was caught, he, in turn was "IT."

Children often preferred to play the game rather than be "IT." Sometimes this was a controversial issue which was resolved in the following manner: All players placed their hands on a table or other flat surface with fingers wide spread. Another player tapped each finger as they chanted:
William Trimble Toes, he's a good fisherman.
Catches fish, puts them in a dish,
Catches hens, puts them in pens.
Wire, blyer, limber lock

Three geese in a flock
One flew east, one flew west,
One flew over the cuckoo's nest. O-U-T spells out goes she (or he).

Needle's Eye:

Two players raise their arms high and clasp their hands to form an arch. All players troop through the arch as the following song is sung:

Needle's eye that doth supply the thread that runs so truly,
Many a beau have I let go because I wanted-YOU.

The object of the game is to catch a player at the end of the song as he (she) is going through the needle's eye.

I Sail My Ship, or Going To California:

The first player says, "I sail my ship loaded with apples, (ants, arabs, etc.).
The second player says, "I sail my ship loaded with beans, (bears, beds, etc.).
The third player says, "I sail my ship loaded with cabbage, (chairs, cucumbers, etc.).
And so on down through the alphabet. Many of the answers bring peals of laughter as the children vision ships loaded with unlikely objects.

Heavy, Heavy, Hangs Over Thy Head:

One person collects an object from each player. A judge is appointed to decree the act each player must perform before he can redeem his article. The first player is blindfolded and seated in a chair. The judge stands behind the chair holding the forfeited article over the head of a player. He then asks, "Is it fine, or super fine?" The person who has collected the article either says, "It is fine," meaning it belongs to a boy, or "It is super-fine," meaning it belongs to a girl. The judge then assessed the penalty for redeeming the article. He may have the player run around the house three times, sing a song, recite a poem, or sometimes, as kissing games were popular, he might tell the player to kiss his sweetheart.

Build The Bridge:

A boy and a girl stand facing each other with arms extended and hands clasped to form an arch. The girl chooses a second boy who walks under the arch and kisses the girl as he passes by. Then he takes his position by the side of the girl, locking his arms with hers and calls the name of another girl. The girl kisses boy No. 1 as she passes through the arch, then locks her arms into his and clasps hands with her partner so forming the second span of the bridge. The boy whose name she calls kisses both girls and locks arms with girl No. 2 after which he calls a third partner and so on. The completed bridge has as many spans as there are couples in the game and the last few couples to line up certainly have a lot of kissing to do.

Club Fist:

Club Fist is played by the first person making a fist, thumb sticking up. The second player grasps the thumb and also makes a fist with thumb sticking up, and so on with each player. The person whose fist is on the bottom removes it and says, "Do you want to take it off?" "Let me knock it off," or "Let the birds peck it off?" The object of the game is to remove all the fists by one means or another. Letting the "birds peck it off" was sometimes pretty painful.

Jump Rope Chants

Cinderella, dressed in yellow, went upstairs to kiss her fellow
By mistake, she kissed a snake, how many doctors will it take?
One - two - three, etc.

Mexico, texico, over the hill to Mexico
Do the splits, do the kicks,
Turn around, get out of town.

I like coffee, I like tea
I like the boys, and they like me.

Teddy Bear, teddy bear, turn around
Teddy Bear, teddy bear, touch the ground
Teddy Bear, teddy bear, get out of town.

Grace, Grace, dressed in lace, went upstairs to powder her face
How many boxes did it take?
One - Two - Three, etc.

Teddy Bear, teddy bear, turn around.
 Teddy Bear, teddy bear, touch the ground
Teddy Bear, teddy bear show your shoes,
Teddy Bear, teddy bear, you're excused.

Hot pepper meant turning the rope very fast.

Epilogue

The walk down the Wire Road in the Missouri Ozarks is over. The last weary Cherokee, resigned to his fate, has found a new home in the West; the swash-buckling stagecoaches of the Tipton, Missouri to San Francisco, California; cannons which meted out death and destruction forever silent; even Route 66, the road of hope for destitute families during the bleak days of the Great Depression has been replaced by the fast moving Interstate highways. It is evident that those who walked the old road in by-gone days will never travel this way again.

Yet even as we record the above events, life moves on. Plans for the future are already under way; the Trail of Tears will be commemorated by markers along existing highways; the Butterfield Overland Mail has already been recognized by a Centennial Anniversary Celebration in 1958; re-enactment or the Battle of Wilson's Creek, which played such an important role in the lives of the settlers along the Wire Road, marked the one hundred thirtieth anniversary of that decisive battle in August 1991; Route 66 is now being marked with the familiar shield from Chicago to Santa Monica, California.

On our walk down the Wire Road in the Missouri Ozarks, we have sought to record history-making events as well as customs and traditions of every day living. Accomplishing this, the mission of writing this book will have been fulfilled.

Continuing Fern's walk of nostalgia, events have moved forward with the year 2000 finding a national event at Wilson's Creek. Other re-enactments at Cassville, Pea Ridge, Fayetteville and Prairie Grove Arkansas being conducted on a near regular basis of places of the past that events happened on the Wire Road

Many houses have been built and continue to be built that takes away the signs of there ever being a Wire Road. So with this in mind we decided to keep the history alive for another period of time so people who follow our steps will realize the historical significance of the past and the Old Wire Road. twr

Bibliography

1. Cassville Republican - June 1958, Butterfield Overland Mail.
2. Cassville Republican - Map of Barry County, Butterfield Overland Mail - Map drawn by Austin Brock, December 30, 1956.
3. Stone County Publishing Company - Information from stories by Leonard Williams and Helen McCord McCoy.
4. National Archives - Special File, 249 - Bureau of Indian Affairs - Diary of Conductor B. B. Cannon.
5. Joint Collection University Western Historical Manuscripts - Diaries of Conductors Dr. W. I. I. Morrow and Rev. Daniel S. Buttrick.
6. Collection Columbia State Historical Society of Missouri Manuscripts.
7. Removal of the Cherokee Indians - John S. Kochtitzky - 1837-1839.
8. Removal of the Cherokee Indians, 1838-1839 - Otto Koenig.
9. Regional Library, Jackson, Missouri; permission to print the Kochtitzky and Koenig papers, by Mildred Seabeodt, Library Co-ordinator.
10. National Archives; Post Masters of the Curran Post Office.
11. Springfield News and Leader, map of Butterfield Overland Mail by Bob Palmer.
12. The Billings Times - The Charles Angus Story.
13. Bittersweet Inc., Ellen Gray Massey, Advisor, sketches of thong trees.
14. Wilson's Creek National Battlefield Park - Permission to use Battlefield Tour Map material.
15. Ozark Mountaineer; editor Clay Anderson; Information on First Telegraph Line by F. P. Rose.
16. McCullah - Wasson 100th Anniversary Edition: Information on McCullah family.
17. The Kansas City Star, April 12, 1959: Sketch of Oxbow Route of Butterfield Overland Mail.
18. Map of Trail of Tears Memorial Highway: Springfield News and Leader, Nov. 7, 1988.
19. National Park Service: National Historical Trail, U. S. Department of the Interior, National Park Service.

Acknowledgements

In appreciation to all who have given so graciously of their time, records, pictures, and memories during the preparation of this book, a sincere "Thank You!"

First of all to my family and especially to my daughter, Mary Lou McCutchan, for her encouragement and support. To the following persons who knew of my desire to write the book and said, "Sure, you can do it!" To Ellen Gray Massey, Lebanon, who helped with the editing process; to Larry Bangle who took time from his busy schedule to draw the beautiful cover; Carley Ann Andrus, journalism teacher and friend; Doug Murphy, whose burning desire to learn more about the old road motivated me anew; Le Roy and Maxine Armstrong and the Life in the Ozarks class; Lois Mounce, author; Jere Krakow, National Park Historian, Denver, Colorado; and to the following friends: Dorothy Roden, Ruth Asher, Juanita Edgar, Elaine Skogman, Tom Lawing, Irene Langley, Virginia Snyder, Mary Hair, Flossie Thompson, Mary Lois Kelley, Emma Lou Hair Barnett, Marjorie Thornton, Helen Spellman and Delores Shively. Last, but not least, to the memory of my late friend, Evert Lee Hair, Sr. He wanted to live to be 100 years old—he almost made it. Another of Evert's wishes was to see the history of the Wire Road recorded for future generations; we have tried hard to do this in the book.

To all of these and many more we say simply, "Thank You!"